FIRST CERTIFICATE

PRACTICE

TESTS

*Five tests for the new
Cambridge First Certificate
in English*

MARK HARRISON • ROSALIE KERR

WITH ANSWERS

OXFORD UNIVERSITY PRESS

Oxford University Press
Great Clarendon Street, Oxford OX2 6DP

Oxford New York

Athens Auckland Bangkok Bogota Bombay Buenos Aires
Calcutta Cape Town Dar es Salaam Delhi Florence Hong Kong
Istanbul Karachi Kuala Lumpur Madras Madrid Melbourne
Mexico City Nairobi Paris Singapore Taipei Tokyo Toronto

and associated companies in
Berlin Ibadan

OXFORD and OXFORD ENGLISH
are trade marks of Oxford University Press

ISBN 0 19 453311 5

With Answers edition
ISBN 0 19 453312 3

© Oxford University Press 1996

First published 1996
Second impression 1997

Printed in Hong Kong

Acknowledgements
The authors and publisher are grateful to those who have given
permission to reproduce the following extracts and adaptations of
copyright material:
p8 Extract from Linford Christie: 'An Autobiography' with kind
permission of the author
p10 from Jennifer Thomson: 'On Camera' and p82 from Mary Johns:
'Queen of the Liners' © The Lady
p13 'Supermarkets, their Secrets Revealed', feature courtesy of
Family Circle and SuperMarketing Magazine
p18 Extract from The Taste of Britain by Marc and Kim Million ©
Marc and Kim Million
p29 Adapted from Ian Morton: 'London and the Car Facing the 21st
Century' © London Evening Standard/Solo Syndications
p30 from Gillian Mercer: 'Surely That's Not the Real Me?' and p32
from Simon Walsh:'And it all went Swimmingly Well' © The
Independent 1994
p35 From Book Case 'Encounters with Famous Novelists' and p38
'Eyewitness Guides' with kind permission of WH Smith
p40 Extract from 'Absolute Beginners', Natural Choice Magazine,
published by Media Partners CPR
p51 Extract from The Post Office Customer Charter with kind
permission of The Post Office
p52 From John Bungey 'How To Write a Best Seller' in Midweek, with
kind permission of the author
p57 'Personal Facts' and p104 Extract from Simon Buckby: 'Brain
Busters' © Girl About Town 1994
p60 From David Rhys Jones: 'Bowled over by Champions of Every
Age' and p62 James Henderson: 'Calypso Fun with a Barb' © Times
Newspapers Limited 1994

p66 Adapted from David Robinson: 'White Magic' Times Magazine ©
Times Newspapers Limited 1994
p73 'Is Noise Driving you Mad?' adapted from Good Housekeeping
© National Magazine Company
p74 Extract from 'Felicia's Journey' by William Trevor, reprinted by
permission of the Peters Fraser & Dunlop Group Ltd
p79 Adapted from 'Do You Know Your Consumer Rights?' Consumer
Magazine, by kind permission of the Consumers' Association
p84 From Liz Holliday 'Stranger than Fiction' © Essentials 1992
p88 Adapted from Jan Duncan-John: 'Wise Women to Modern
Medics' with kind permission of the author
p95 From Verity Watkins: 'Decisions, Decisions' © 19 Magazine/
Robert Harding Syndication
p96 From 'Get to Grips with your Thermals' © Ms London 1994
p98 Adapted from Mike Gerrard: 'Foot Notes' © Times Newpapers
Limited, 1994
p106 Extract from Recycling Leaflet, by permission of the Steel
Recycling Centre
p153 Adapted from Tony Williams interviewed by Simon Bates (LBC
4.7.94) by permission of Jeffrey Simmons

Although every effort has been made to trace and contact copyright
holders before publication, this has not been possible in these
cases. We apologize for any apparent infringement of copyright and
if notified, the publisher will be pleased to rectify any errors or
omissions at the earliest opportunity.

p7 From Amber Kennedy: 'Fresh Start' from Chic Magazine 1994
p16 'Garrett A Morgan' from The Guardian
p22 Suellen Bizub: 'Autumn Shape-Up' in Nine to Five
p44 Road Maps from Sue Baker:'Cars and Bikes' in Observer Life
p54 From Safari Park Keepers, Careers Library Service
p76 Alan Brack: 'A Better Class of Musical', author untraced
p110 Extract from Alistair Aird: 'The Good Weekend Guide', Peters
Fraser and Dunlop Group

The authors and publisher are grateful to the University of
Cambridge Local Examinations Syndicate for permission to
reproduce the sample answer sheets on pages 116–119 and the
Paper 2 marking information on page 139.

The publisher would also like the following for their permission to
reproduce photographs on pages 120–128:
Ace Photo Agency; Clive Barda; John Birdsall Photography;
Britstock IFA; Eye Ubiquitous; The Hutchison Library; The Image
Bank; Yiorgos Nikiteas; Performing Arts Library; Sporting Pictures
(UK); Tony Stone Images; Stewart Weir.

Illustrations by:
Judy Stevens.

The authors and publisher would also like to thank Val Hennessy
and Jackie Martin for their valuable comments and suggestions at
manuscript stage.

The tests were piloted with several groups of FCE students. The
staff and students of the following schools and colleges deserve
special thanks for participating in the trialling phase and providing
the sample student answers on pages 140–144:
Anglo World, London; Chichester College of Arts, Science and
Technology; Clarendon College, Nottingham; English Language
Training, London; Eurocentre, London; Frances King, London;
International Language Academy, London; Language Project,
Bristol; Multi Lingua, Guildford.

Contents

Introduction

This book contains five complete practice tests for the revised First Certificate in English (FCE), Cambridge Level 3. Developed by experienced writers, the tests accurately reflect the coverage and level of the real examination. Each of the texts in Papers 1 and 3 has been taken from a different source, in order to include examples of the wide variety of text types that you may find in the actual examination.

Note: In Papers 1, 3 and 4, you have to write your answers on special answer sheets. See pages 116-119 for examples of these.

The five FCE Papers are described in detail below. Page references to a relevant example of each particular task type are included after the symbol → .

Paper 1 Reading (1 hour 15 minutes)

In this paper, there are four parts and 35 questions in all. Reading texts are taken from a range of sources, including newspapers, magazines, leaflets, brochures, advertisements or books. Note that in Part 2 the text may also be taken from a short story, novel, biography or autobiography.

PART 1 Matching

You will read a text that is divided into 7 or 8 sections and be asked to do one of the following tasks:

- choose which heading is appropriate for each section → 6-7
- choose which sentence best summarizes each section → 28-29

In either case, you will have to answer 6 or 7 questions and you will be given a list of possible answers to choose from. There will be one extra heading or sentence that is not the answer to any question and is not used. You will be given the answer for the first section as an example.

PART 2 Multiple choice

You will read a text and be asked to answer 7 or 8 multiple choice questions about it. For each question, you must choose A, B, C or D.

Most of the questions will ask about the details in the text. Other questions may ask about these aspects:

- references in the text, for example *What does 'it' in line 18 refer to?* → 8-9
- particular words and phrases used in the text, for example *What does the writer mean by 'judgemental' in the fifth paragraph?* → 30-31
- the text as a whole, for example *What is the purpose of the article?* → 52-53

PART 3 Gapped text

You will read a text from which 7 or 8 sentences or paragraphs have been removed. The missing sentences or paragraphs will be printed on the opposite page and you must decide where they fit in the text. There will always be one extra sentence or paragraph that does not fit anywhere. You will be given the first answer as an example.

- missing sentences → 10-11
- missing paragraphs → 32-33

PART 4 Matching

You will read a text or a series of short texts and have to answer between 13 and 15 questions. You will be asked to do one of the following tasks:

- match a list of statements, references or opinions to the sections of the text in which they appear → 12-13
- match a list of statements, references or opinions to people or things mentioned in the text → 34-35; 56-57
- match a list of statements, references or opinions to information given in the text → 78-79

There may be only one correct answer to a question. However, sometimes more than one answer is required and this will be indicated. Where this is the case, answers may be given in any order. You will be given the first answer as an example.

Occasionally, there may also be one or two multiple choice questions of a general type, which ask about the text as a whole.

Paper 2 Writing (1 hour 30 minutes)

This paper has two parts of equal importance. Part 1 is a compulsory task for all candidates. In Part 2, you must select one task from a choice of four. For each part, you will be expected to write between 120 and 180 words, making a total of between 240 and 360 words for the whole paper.

PART 1

For Question 1 you have to write a 'transactional' letter, that is, a letter written in response to a situation and itself giving rise to further action. You are asked to read up to three short texts, such as letters, adverts, postcards and extracts from diaries or articles. There are sometimes additional visual prompts, such as drawings or photographs. All of this material, which is never more than 250 words long, gives you information about a situation. You then have to respond by writing a suitable letter.

Your letter should be almost entirely based on the information given to you and you are not expected to draw on your own knowledge or imagination. Neither are you asked to take on the character of another person in order to write the letter. You are given the situation and should respond to it as you would in real life.

The type of language you will have to use in your letter may include, for example, the language of explaining, suggesting, complaining, describing, apologizing, reporting, persuading and giving and asking for advice and information. You should write in a style that is appropriate for the specified reader of the letter:

- a formal letter → 14; 80
- an informal letter → 36; 58

PART 2

The choice of questions in Part 2 should provide you with an opportunity to write about something related to your own interests and experience. All Paper 2 tasks state a context within which you are expected to write and there is a genuine purpose for writing. You will be given information about the target reader and you should think about the effect you wish your piece of writing to have on that reader.

Questions 2, 3 and 4 may be writing tasks of the following kinds:

- an informal letter → 15; 81
- a letter of application → 37; 59
- an article → 37; 103
- a report → 59; 81
- a composition → 81; 103
- a short story → 15; 59

These tasks are usually presented through the rubric, which is never more than 70 words long.

Question 5 consists of a choice of two tasks related to one of five 'background reading texts'. Both tasks are of a general nature, in that they may be related to any of the five texts. The tasks are of similar types to those mentioned above. The background reading texts for December 1996 are:

Oxford Bookworm Collections *Crime Never Pays*
E. M. Forster *A Passage to India*
Aldous Huxley *Brave New World*
Daphne du Maurier *Rebecca*
G.B. Shaw *Pygmalion*

MARKING INFORMATION

Paper 2 is marked by trained examiners, who are usually teachers. The answer to each part is assessed according to a number of criteria, including the content of the piece of writing; the accuracy of vocabulary, structure, spelling and punctuation; the range of vocabulary and structure; the organization and cohesion of the piece of writing; the appropriacy of the register and the general effect on the target reader.

The UCLES General Mark Scheme for Paper 2 is reproduced on page 139 of the 'With Answers' edition. Though correct at time of going to press, it is likely to be subject to revision.

Detailed descriptions of suitable answers to the tasks in this book are given in the Key on pages 129-138 of the 'With Answers' edition. There are also sample student answers for the Part 1 tasks on pages 140-144.

Paper 3 Use of English (1 hour 15 minutes)

In this paper, there are five parts and 65 questions in all. The texts are taken from a variety of sources, including newspaper or magazine articles, brochures, leaflets, advertisements or books. Texts for Part 4 may also be letters, reports or stories and may include the language of description or opinion.

PART 1 Multiple choice cloze

In this part, you will be tested mainly on vocabulary. You will read a short text with gaps in it. For each gap, you will be given four words or short phrases and you must choose which one fills the gap correctly. You will have to decide one of the following:

● which word or phrase fits in the context of what is said
● which word goes together with the other words or completes a phrase
● which word or phrase correctly links parts of a sentence
● which phrasal verb fits the meaning of what is said

You will be given the first answer as an example and will have to answer 15 questions. → 16-17

PART 2 Open cloze

In this part, you will be tested mainly on grammar. You will read a text with gaps in it. You must fill each of the gaps with one word only. You will not be given any words to choose from. The word that you write will do one of the following:

● complete the meaning of the sentence
● complete a phrase
● go together with other words
● link the meaning within a sentence
● complete a phrasal verb

You will be given the first answer as an example and will have to answer 15 questions. → 18

PART 3 Key word transformations

In this part, you will be tested both on grammatical structures and lexical phrases. There are 10 questions. For each question, you will be given a sentence and asked to complete a second sentence so that it has a similar meaning to the first one. You will be given a word that you must use when completing the second sentence. You cannot change this word. You must use no more than five words to complete the sentence, including the word you are given.

You will be given an example at the beginning. → 19-20

PART 4 Error correction

This part focuses on grammar. You will read a short text which contains some errors. The text will be presented as 17 numbered lines. Some of the lines will be correct and you must tick these on your answer sheet. The other lines will be incorrect because they contain one extra word which should not be there. For these lines, you will have to write the extra word on your answer sheet.

You will be given examples of both a correct and an incorrect line. You will have to answer 15 questions. → 21

PART 5 Word formation

This part focuses on vocabulary. You will read a short text which contains gaps in most or all of its lines. Next to each gapped line there will be a word in capital letters. You must form another word from this word to fill the gap.

You will be given the first answer as an example. You will have to answer 10 questions. → 22

Paper 4 Listening (about 40 minutes)

The listening test lasts approximately 35 minutes. You are then given five minutes to transfer your answers to your answer sheet. There are four parts and 30 questions in all. You will hear each part twice.

PART 1 Short extracts

You will hear 8 short, unrelated pieces of about 30 seconds each. There may be one or two speakers. For each piece you will be asked one multiple choice question, for which you will be given three choices, A, B or C. Each question and its choices are also recorded on the tape.

The questions will test your understanding of a number of things, for example:

● who is speaking
● what the speaker's purpose is
● what the topic or situation is
● what feeling or opinion is expressed
● details of what is said

You will have to answer 8 questions. → 23

PART 2 Note-taking

You will hear a piece lasting approximately three minutes. There will be one or more speakers. The questions are presented in the form of notes or sentences and test your understanding of the information you hear. You will have to write a word or short phrase for each question.

You will have to answer 10 questions. → 24

PART 3 Matching

You will hear five short pieces, each lasting about 30 seconds. There may be one or two speakers in each piece. You will be asked to match a list of choices to the five pieces. You will be given 6 choices in all, but one of these choices does not answer any of the questions.

You will have to answer 5 questions. → 25

PART 4 Selecting from two or three possible answers

In this part of the test you will hear one piece, which will last for about three minutes. There will be one, two or three speakers. The questions will be one of the following types:

● multiple choice with three choices → 26
● yes/no or true/false questions → 48
● matching questions, asking, for example, which speaker said what → 92

You will have to answer 7 questions.

Paper 5 Speaking (about 15 minutes for two candidates)

This paper consists of four parts and the tasks focus on giving and exchanging information and opinions. The usual format is an interview with two candidates and two examiners present. In certain circumstances, it may be possible for a candidate to have an individual interview. When this is the case, the length of the interview is 9-10 minutes and there is only one examiner present. In Parts 2, 3 and 4, the examiner takes the place of the second candidate in discussions.

During a paired interview, one of the two examiners acts only as an assessor and does not join in the conversation. The other examiner acts as an assessor and 'interlocutor', that is, he or she speaks to the candidates and manages the interview.

PART 1

Here you will speak mainly to the interlocutor, who will ask you some questions about yourself. This part lasts about 4 minutes.

PART 2

In this part, you will be given two pictures and asked to talk about them for approximately one minute. The other candidate will then be given a brief opportunity to add his or her comments about your pictures, before being given two new pictures to talk about for the same length of time. You will then be given a brief opportunity to comment on the other candidate's pictures. This part lasts about 4 minutes in total.

PART 3

In this part, you will be given a set of pictures or a drawing to look at with the other candidate. You will be given a related task and you will have a discussion together. This Part lasts about 3 minutes.

PART 4

In this final part of the interview, you will discuss various questions related to the topic of Part 3 with the other candidate and the interlocutor, sharing your views and justifying your opinions. This part lasts about 4 minutes.

ASSESSMENT

In the interview, you will be assessed on your use of grammar and vocabulary, your pronunciation and your ability to communicate effectively in discussion with other people.

Test 1

Paper 1 Reading (1 hour 15 minutes)

PART 1

You are going to read a magazine article about changing your life. Choose the most suitable heading from the list **A–H** for each part (**1–6**) of the article. There is one extra heading which you do not need to use. There is an example at the beginning (**0**).
Mark your answers **on the separate answer sheet**.

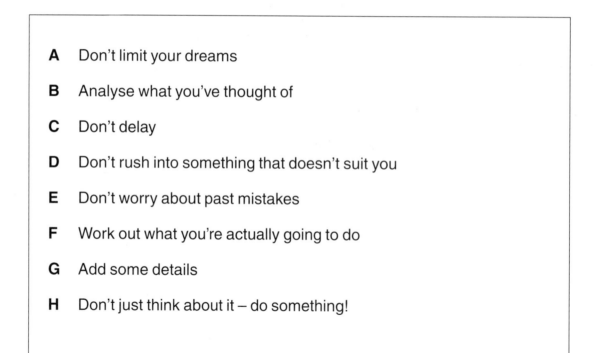

A   Don't limit your dreams

B   Analyse what you've thought of

C   Don't delay

D   Don't rush into something that doesn't suit you

E   Don't worry about past mistakes

F   Work out what you're actually going to do

G   Add some details

H   Don't just think about it – do something!

Fresh Start

0	*H*

Knowing that we want to make a change in our lives is the easy bit – deciding what to do and how to do it is more difficult. First of all, we must learn to take our dreams seriously and to trust our abilities. Old habits die hard, and fear of failure may prevent us from even trying something new.

1	

Making a fresh start takes effort – and time. It is important to think carefully before you set off into something new, because it must be right for you and your way of life. You will need determination to overcome the problems that are sure to arise and the crises of confidence that you will face, so be sure that it's something *you* want to do – not what you think you *can* do, or what someone else thinks you *should* do.

2	

Before you begin to think of specific projects, let your imagination fly beyond the here and now and think about what, in an ideal world, you would really love to do. This should help you to get in touch with the real you beneath the daily worries that drag you down. Don't let lack of money, time, qualifications or any other negative reasons why you cannot do what you want stand in the way of your fantasies. The time for assessing real possibilities will come later, when the various options can be considered in a systematic way.

Imagining the impossible need not be a waste of time. Such flights of fancy can provide clues as to where you would like to be, or what you might want to work towards. Try the following exercise. Imagine for a time that there are no restrictions for you of time, money, age, status, ties, etc. Then select one of the following – MY FANTASY JOB; MY FANTASY DAY; MY FANTASY LIFE.

3	

Think through your chosen topic and write down your version of what would be involved. For example, in your fantasy job identify things such as status, salary, job specification, style of work, the lifestyle which accompanies it, with whom you would work and in what surroundings. Your fantasy day is an invitation to list the events of what for you would be the 'perfect day'. Where would you be, what would you do, and with whom, if anybody? Your fantasy life offers an opportunity to consider your ideal life as a whole. This picture would include the work pattern, combining work, home and social life, status, income, lifestyle, etc. Whichever topic you choose, put in as many of the particulars as you can so that the fantasy becomes a full picture.

4	

When you have written down your fantasy, think carefully through the following:

- What are my reactions to doing the exercise? What does the fantasy indicate about what I want for myself?

- What are the differences between my fantasy and my reality?

- How much of my fantasy is achievable at present or might be in the future? If I can't have it all, can I have some of it?

- What are the barriers to my achieving some of my fantasy and how might these be overcome?

- What would be the consequences of my working to achieve some of the features of my fantasy, for myself and for other people?

- Would the pursuit of my fantasy be worth the possible consequences? What objectives would I like to set myself on the basis of this exercise?

5	

You then need to identify your strengths and weaknesses, update old skills or learn new ones. Look at your resources and, perhaps most important, what you enjoy and what you really can't bear doing. Be specific about your goals, and be careful not to try to do too much.

6	

When you have decided what your goal is, and all the thinking, planning and preparation has been done, your fresh start can no longer be put off. Ban negative thoughts and seize the moment – fresh starters are determined to see the positive side of things and not to let problems, real or imagined, block their path. Good luck!

PART 2

You are going to read an extract from a book. For questions **7–14**, choose the answer (**A, B, C** or **D**) which you think fits best according to the text.
Mark your answers **on the separate answer sheet**.

They call Jamaica the 'Island in the Sun', and that is my memory of it. Of sunshine, warmth and abundant fruit growing everywhere, and of love. I was born on 2 April 1960 in St Andrews in Kingston. There were two sisters ahead of me in the family, and though of course I didn't know it, there was excited talk of emigration, possibly to Canada but more usually to England, the land of opportunity. I guess that plans were already being made when I was born, for a year or so later my Dad left for London. Two years after that, when he had saved enough money, my Mum went as well and my sisters and I were left in the care of my grandmother. I stayed with her, in her house near the centre of Kingston, until I was seven years old. My grandmother, therefore, shaped my life, and I believe I am all the better for it.   5

This was all fairly normal. Emigrating to better yourself was a dream for most Jamaicans, a dream many were determined to fulfil. Families were close and grandmothers were an important part of family life so, when the mass emigrations began, it seemed perfectly right and natural for them to take over the running of the families left behind.   10
After all, they had the experience.

Grandmothers are often strict, but they usually also spoil you. At least, that is the way it was with mine. She ran the family like a military operation: each of us, no matter how young, had our tasks. I remember that we didn't have a tap in the house, but used a communal tap from which we had to fill two barrels in our garden. Every morning, before we went to school, we all had to take a bucket appropriate to our size and run a relay from the communal tap to the barrels until   15
they were full. In the beginning, when I was two or three, I couldn't reach the barrel – but I still had to join in. My sisters had to sweep the yard before they went to school. My grandmother would give orders to the eldest and these were passed down – as I got older I found this particularly annoying! But I can tell you, no one avoided their duties.

My Dad came over from England to see how we were getting on. I hadn't known him when he had left for Britain, but when I saw him I somehow knew that he was my father. He talked to us about the new country, about snow, about the   20
huge city, and we all wanted to know more, to see what it was like. He also told me that I now had a younger brother, which made me feel excited and wonder what he could be like. I didn't know it at the time, but he had come to prepare us for the move to England. Six months later my grandmother told me that I was going to join my parents and that she, too, was emigrating. It was the end of my time in the Caribbean, of the sheltered, warm, family life that I had known there, and the beginning of a new and exciting era.   25

London was strange and disappointing. There was no gold on the pavements, as the stories in Jamaica had indicated. Back home it had always been warm. Everyone was friendly and said 'Hello' when you passed by on the street; in Kingston you knew everybody and they knew you. Here, it wasn't like that. The roads were busy, the buildings were grey and dull, with many tall, high-rise blocks. It was totally unlike Jamaica, the houses all small and packed close together. In my grandmother's house I had a big bedroom; here I had to share. At that age it was a great disappointment.   30

Worse was to come, because there followed a very cold winter, and I had never felt cold in my life before. Then came the biggest shock: snow. White flakes came out of the sky and Dad smiled, pointed and said, 'That's snow!' I rushed outside, looked up and opened my mouth to let the flakes drop in. The snow settled on my tongue and it was so cold that I cried. My toes lost all feeling, and at the primary school that we attended I wasn't allowed to wear long trousers at my age. The teachers made us go out to play in the playground and I joined in with all the fun, sliding around in the snow,   35
throwing snowballs, all the usual things. Suddenly, as my shoes and socks got soaking wet and frozen, there came an excruciating pain and I cried with the intensity of it. I didn't know what was happening to me.

7 The writer says that when he was very young,

    A he was upset because his parents left.

    B he was very keen to go to England.

    C his parents had decided to leave.

    D his parents changed their plans.

8 According to the writer, many people from Jamaica at that time

    A wanted to be free from responsibility.

    B had ambitions that were unrealistic.

    C wanted to improve their standard of living.

    D disliked the country they came from.

9 The writer says that when he lived with his grandmother

    A he was treated like the other children.

    B he wanted to be like the other children.

    C he tried to avoid doing certain duties.

    D he found some of her rules strange.

10 What does 'this' in line 18 refer to?

    A being told what to do by his sisters

    B having to sweep the yard before school

    C having to do duties he found difficult

    D being given orders by his grandmother

11 What happened when the writer's father came?

    A His father did not tell him why he had come.

    B He did not know how to react to his father.

    C His father told him things that were untrue.

    D He felt anxious about what his father told him.

12 When the writer first went to London, he was disappointed because

    A it was smaller than he had expected.

    B he had been given a false impression of it.

    C he had to spend a lot of time on his own.

    D his new surroundings frightened him.

13 What does the writer say about snow?

    A He was not sure how to react when he saw it.

    B He regretted coming into contact with it.

    C He was embarrassed that it made him cry.

    D He was not very keen to touch it.

14 Which of the following would be the best title for this passage?

    A Too Many Changes.

    B A Strange Childhood.

    C Hard Times.

    D From Sun To Snow.

PART 3

You are going to read a magazine article. Eight sentences have been removed from the article. Choose from the sentences **A–I** the one which fits each gap (**15–21**). There is one extra sentence which you do not need to use. There is an example at the beginning (**0**).

Mark your answers **on the separate answer sheet**.

On camera

When I saw the notice 'Women film extras wanted' in a local newspaper, I jumped at the chance. As a child I had dreamt of being a film star. **0** | *I* |

The casting interview, held in a church hall with many budding actors in attendance, went well, and two days later I was told that I had been chosen. The production in question was revealed as Scottish Television's *Dr Finlay* drama, which is set in the 1950s.

15 | Extras are often left in the dark for some time when it comes to being told which role they will play. Finally, the nature of my role was revealed; I was asked to play a mental hospital patient.

16 | Then, barely a week later, the day of filming dawned. All 13 of us extras, mainly housewives, were told to change into our costumes in the wardrobe department. Then we were driven to the location, a hospital on the fringes of Glasgow. It seems that it is common for old hospitals to be used in this way.

On arriving, we were given coffee and tea, which looked and tasted like cement. Then we were rushed off to make-up. My hair was pinned back and make-up was applied that gave me a pale appearance. Then we were sent to the minibus for a few hours, as the cameras rolled elsewhere.

After the second hour had passed I was becoming bored. **17** | I had expected to be so busy that I hadn't come prepared for a long wait. Many of the others had brought a book or knitting.

Three hours had now passed. **18** | A large room in the hospital had been transformed into a dayroom for that purpose. Although I had expected the room to be warm because of the lighting equipment present, it was quite chilly.

When the director came in, we were instructed what to do and where to stand. Along with a few others, I was told to sit at a table and weave baskets. **19** | The cane we had to use was very long. On several occasions my basket fell apart in front of my very eyes. On others I only succeeded in hitting a cameraman in the eye.

20 | Jean, who was barefoot, had to circle the floor. Poor Alice was asked to pretend to bang her head against the wall. Meanwhile, Veronica swept the floor.

Thankfully, after just a few attempts, the scenes were done. **21** | Although I found the experience very interesting, my first screen role will almost certainly be my last.

A   This was not an easy task.

B   Life for the other extras was far from easy.

C   So some things just aren't meant to happen, I suppose.

D   Despite my disappointment, I agreed to participate.

E   And so my first taste of this 'glamorous' career was over.

F   I was to lose some of my enthusiasm for the idea, however.

G   I bet stars are never treated like this, I thought.

H   Then at last we were called to do our scenes.

I   Now at last I would get my chance.

PART 4

You are going to read an article about supermarkets. For questions **22–35**, choose from the sections of the article (**A–E**). Some of the sections may be chosen more than once. When more than one answer is required, these may be given in any order. There is an example at the beginning (**0**).
Mark your answers **on the separate answer sheet**.

Which section refers to:

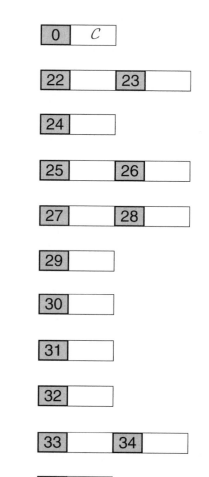

an arrangement between producers and supermarkets?	**0**	*C*
the order in which customers buy goods?	**22**	**23**
customers consuming goods they have bought?	**24**	
a method that may have the opposite effect to the one intended?	**25**	**26**
customers having the wrong idea about something?	**27**	**28**
goods getting damaged?	**29**	
supermarkets being reorganized?	**30**	
matching something to particular types of customer?	**31**	
not putting certain types of goods together?	**32**	
supermarkets paying attention to customers' comments?	**33**	**34**
a system that may die out?	**35**	

SUPERMARKETS
Their secrets revealed ...

Have you ever wondered why some stores smell of fresh bread or why some play music and others don't? We asked the experts at SuperMarketing magazine to explain some of the hidden tricks of the trade.

A Fresh start

'Why are the fresh fruit and vegetables usually at the entrance to the store? It's always crowded, and they get squashed if I have to load heavy cans and packets on top.'

It's simply because supermarkets make a high profit on fresh fruit and vegetables, and they have discovered they sell more of them if they're near the entrance. According to research carried out by supermarkets, customers prefer fresh goods to come first. Maybe it's because many of us arrive at the store concentrating on the kinds of fruit and vegetable we need. Once we've got that out of the way, we can relax and do the rest of the shopping at leisure. Another reason is that if we see fresh goods first, the sight and smell of all those rosy apples and glossy aubergines give a 'feel good' impression of freshness and quality which we carry around the store.

Nowadays, trolleys should have a separate compartment where you can place fruit and vegetables so they don't get squashed.

B On the scent

'Do they have to pipe smells of freshly baked bread around stores? I always end up buying an extra loaf or cake because the smell is just so tempting.'

That's what the store is counting on! It's well-known in the retail food industry that smell is the most powerful of human senses when it comes to influencing our choice of where we shop and what we buy. For years, some stores have been piping smells of freshly baked bread and real coffee through the air-conditioning to get appetites going. But this may be counterproductive, the retail consultants Retail Dynamics point out: 'If you are doing your shopping at lunch or dinner-time, when you are already hungry, the smell of baking may send you straight to the bread counter and then out of the store so you can eat quickly.'

C All change

'Why is it that supermarkets change their layout so often? Just when I have speeded up my shopping by knowing where everything is, they move the section!'

This is another way of trying to make you buy things you thought you didn't need. Supermarkets make most of their money out of fresh foods and 'luxury' snacks and far less on essentials like milk, sugar and bread. So everyday items are scattered around the store because in order to get them, you have to pass the 'high earners' and, hopefully, suddenly decide to buy some.

The eye-catching display on the unit at the end of a row does not necessarily mean that the goods are the bargain of the week, as you may think. Manufacturers sometimes pay the supermarket to put their brands in the best positions. Among the best are the places across the ends of units where customer traffic is very high.

D Quick march!

'Why does my supermarket have to play music all the time? It drives me mad and I can't avoid it since it's the only store I can reach conveniently.'

This may be an attempt to please customers – so they will enjoy shopping more – or a way of projecting an image. One supermarket plays 1960s music to go with its decor. Another sets out simply to please – playing 1950s and 1960s music in the morning when older customers do most of their shopping, pop music in the evenings and on Saturdays for a younger audience, and music that appeals to the whole family on a Sunday. Some stores use music to increase their profits by playing slow waltzes or light classics on quiet days, like Mondays, to keep customers browsing and buying. At busier times, like Saturdays, they'll increase the tempo to encourage customers to move quickly through the store.

A recent supermarket study reported a 38% increase in sales when the store played slow music compared to fast. However, you can shop in silence at some supermarkets, which never play music – their customers say it puts them off.

E Last straw

'Why do I always choose the queue that moves the slowest?'

Perhaps you're too considerate! For example, don't think the wider checkouts marked 'disabled' are exclusively for wheelchairs. If there are no wheelchair customers waiting, anyone is welcome to use them. And if you're in a real hurry, avoid the checkout assistant wearing a 'trainee' badge – a sign of possible delay.

Checkouts could become a thing of the past anyway. One supermarket is testing a hand-held unit which customers use themselves as they shop. It reads and records the prices of groceries and then totals the bill ... but you still have to pay before you leave.

Paper 2 Writing (1 hour 30 minutes)

PART 1

You **must** answer this question.

1 You have seen this advertisement for a holiday job in an English-language magazine and want to find out more.

Read carefully the advertisement and the notes you have made. Then write a letter to Mrs Malone, telling her a little bit about yourself and why you want the job, and including all your questions.

What kind of help?

Hours of work?

Pay?

Energetic person needed to join in family holiday.

WE need help with our two lively children during a three-week summer holiday in Scotland.

ages?

dates?

YOU need to practise your English.

Can we help each other? If you think we can, write for further details to Mrs Anne Malone, 30 Pond Road, London SW9 0TT.

Write a **letter** of **120–180** words in an appropriate style. Do not write any addresses.

PART 2

Write an answer to **one** of the questions **2–5** in this part. Write your answer in
120–180 words in an appropriate style, putting the question number in the
box.

---

2   An international magazine for students is asking for suggestions from its readers on how to
dress in an interesting way without spending a lot of money.

Write an **article** for the magazine on this subject, giving your own ideas.

3   Your new pen friend in the USA has asked you to describe your memories of an important
family celebration which took place when you were a child.

Write a **letter** to your pen friend, describing a family celebration you remember.

4   Your English club is running a short story competition. The story must begin with the following
words:

Nothing was ever the same again after that morning when the letter arrived.

The story can be based on something which really happened to you or someone you know, or it
can all come from your imagination.

Write your **story** for the competition.

5   **Background reading texts**

Answer **one** of the following two questions based on your reading of **one** of the set books.
Write the title of the book next to the question number box.

5(a) In the book which you have read, how big a part is played by the city, town or country where the
story takes place? Write an **article** for your college magazine, describing the place and its
importance to the story.

5(b) Describe one of the minor characters in the book which you have read and say why he or she is
necessary to the story.

Paper 3 Use of English (1 hour 15 minutes)

PART 1

For questions **1–15**, read the text below and decide which word or phrase **A, B, C** or **D** best fits each space. There is an example at the beginning (**0**). Mark your answers **on the separate answer sheet**.

Example:

| 0 | **A** observer | **B** viewer | **C** witness | **D** spectator |

| 0 | A | B | C | D |

Garrett A Morgan

An accident between a car and a horse-drawn carriage turned on a green light in the mind of one **(0)** .... to it. Why not, thought Garrett A Morgan, design a signal that would **(1)** .... the movement of road traffic? **(2)** .... a result, in February 1927 Morgan produced the world's first automatic electric traffic signal.

His invention **(3)** .... of a pole with two arms that turned round to **(4)** .... when traffic should move. The words 'stop' and 'go' were on different sides of the arms, which automatically turned and **(5)** .... the right line of traffic when necessary.

Morgan, who had been **(6)** .... about road safety because of the **(7)** .... number of cars coming on to the roads at the **(8)** .... , sold his invention to the General Electric Company for $40,000.

Morgan was born in Kentucky in 1877 and **(9)** .... an elementary education. In 1905 he began a job **(10)** .... sewing machines and in 1907 he **(11)** .... his own shop for this. He **(12)** .... on to start a company selling hair treatments and later he invented the 'safety hood', which **(13)** .... firemen from gas and smoke and **(14)** .... a prize at a 1914 exhibition.

Morgan died in 1963, just months after being **(15)** .... by the US government with an award for inventing the first automatic traffic signal.

1	**A** direct	**B** train	**C** master	**D** rule
2	**A** With	**B** Being	**C** As	**D** By
3	**A** composed	**B** combined	**C** constructed	**D** consisted
4	**A** declare	**B** indicate	**C** sign	**D** inform
5	**A** aimed	**B** opposed	**C** viewed	**D** faced
6	**A** tense	**B** restless	**C** excited	**D** concerned
7	**A** raising	**B** increasing	**C** enlarging	**D** heightening
8	**A** while	**B** period	**C** time	**D** age
9	**A** received	**B** attained	**C** gathered	**D** took
10	**A** remedying	**B** mending	**C** revising	**D** correcting
11	**A** opened	**B** introduced	**C** installed	**D** formed
12	**A** took	**B** went	**C** kept	**D** got
13	**A** covered	**B** prevented	**C** saved	**D** protected
14	**A** reached	**B** caught	**C** won	**D** succeeded
15	**A** respected	**B** honoured	**C** approved	**D** valued

PART 2

For questions **16–30**, read the text below and think of the word which best fits each space. Use only **one** word in each space. There is an example at the beginning (**0**).
Write your word **on the separate answer sheet**.

Example: | **0** | *like* |

The Fish and Chip Shop

Harry Ramsden's is a remarkable establishment in Yorkshire, in the North of England. It looks more (**0**) .... a cinema or fire station than a world-famous restaurant, and it (**16**) .... a symbol of a certain attitude (**17**) .... food in the North of England.

The car park beside (**18**) .... unique place has up to sixteen coaches in (**19**) .... at any time. Numerous cars, too, (**20**) .... every type, size and age, are also parked there. Outside the building, a queue stretches around the side. Those waiting to be seated appear rather anxious, (**21**) .... if they are children waiting to go into a theme park. (**22**) .... is a sense of excitement. Harry Ramsden's is (**23**) .... merely a restaurant: it is an event.

Inside the vast carpeted dining room, elegant glass lights illuminate tables (**24**) .... are laid with simple blue-checked table cloths, ordinary plates, cups and saucers (**25**) .... bottles of sauce. Everyone is there (**26**) .... enjoy the favourite food of the area – fish and chips, cooked to perfection (**27**) .... a unique environment. This simple meal has been served to film stars, politicians and miners alike.

Harry Ramsden's is an English celebration of simple, value-for-money food, served stylishly and enjoyed (**28**) .... all. More Harry Ramsden's restaurants (**29**) .... opened since the original one, (**30**) .... in Britain and abroad.

PART 3

For questions **31–40**, complete the second sentence so that it has a similar meaning to the first sentence. Use the word given and other words to complete each sentence. **You must not write more than five words. Do not change the word given.** There is an example at the beginning (**0**).
Write **only** the missing words **on the separate answer sheet**.

Example:

0 'Do you know how to get to the town centre?' she asked me.

way

She asked me .... to the town centre.

The gap can be filled by the words

| **0** | *whether I knew the way* | OR | **0** | *if I knew the way* |

---

31 We won't get to the airport in less than 30 minutes.

least

It will .... 30 minutes to get to the airport.

32 Despite knowing the area well, I got lost.

even

I got lost .... the area well.

33 I tried to talk to Jack about the problem but he was too busy.

word

I tried to .... about the problem but he was too busy.

34 'I don't mind which film we see,' I said.

matter

I said that .... me which film we saw.

35 If you don't take care of those shoes, they won't last for long.

look

Unless ...., those shoes won't last for long.

36 You've already lied to me once today.

lie

This is not the first .... me today.

37 Did you enjoy the party?

good

Did you .... the party?

38 Whenever I hear this song, I remember the time when I was in Paris.

reminds

Whenever I hear this song, ... the time when I was in Paris.

39 I can't describe people as well as you can.

better

You're .... I am.

40 You didn't think carefully enough before you decided.

ought

You .... more carefully before you decided.

PART 4

For questions **41–55**, read the text below and look carefully at each line. Some of the lines are correct, and some have a word which should not be there.
If a line is correct, put a tick (✓) by the number **on the separate answer sheet**.
If a line has a word which should **not** be there, write the word **on the separate answer sheet**. There are two examples at the beginning (**0**) and (**00**).

Examples:

0	*the*
00	✓

I'm afraid I can't come

0	I've been trying to get in touch with you by the phone for a couple
00	of weeks, but I think there must be something wrong with your phone.
41	It keeps up making a funny noise every time I dial your number, so
42	I thought I'd better write to you instead. The problem is that I won't
43	be able to come and stay with you the next weekend. What has
44	happened it is that my parents have arranged to give a big party for the
45	whole family at that weekend. They told me about it several weeks ago
46	and I promised I would be there. Unfortunately, after I had forgotten all
47	about it when I arranged to come and stay with you. As you probably
48	know, I haven't got a very much good memory! Anyway, I'm very sorry,
49	but I really can't let them down. I hope that this doesn't cause to you too
50	much trouble and that we'll be able to arrange another one weekend when
51	I can come. Please write back and suggest for a date that will suit you, or
52	if your phone is working again, please give me a ring and we can discuss
53	about it. Once again, I apologise for making such a terrible mistake
54	and I hope that you won't be too angry with me. I was really looking
55	forward to spending a weekend with you and I hope so that we'll be able to
	arrange this soon.

PART 5

For questions **56–65**, read the text below. Use the word given in capitals at the end of each line to form a word that fits in the space in the same line. There is an example at the beginning (**0**).
Write your word **on the separate answer sheet**.

Example: | **0** | *depression* |

EXERCISE

Exercise is one of the best ways of keeping (**0**) .... away. It   **DEPRESSED**

improves your body and your mind and (**56**) .... you to perform   **ABLE**

better in the work place and at home.

Proper (**57**) .... is essential if you want to get the most from   **BREATH**

exercise and you should also take into (**58**) .... your heart rate.   **CONSIDER**

It can be (**59**) .... to do too much, which is why all good fitness   **HARM**

instructors emphasise the (**60**) .... of 'listening to your body'.   **IMPORTANT**

When you first start you should use good (**61**) ...., because it's   **JUDGE**

easy to make the mistake of using the equipment (**62**) .... or   **CORRECT**

doing too much at one time. Start slowly and build up gradually.

Exercise should not be seen as a (**63**) .... task; it can be as easy   **DEMAND**

as a quick walk. To increase your fitness (**64**) ...., exercise for 20   **STEADY**

minutes a day, 4 to 6 times a week and you will notice a (**65**) ....   **DIFFERENT**

in your body and mind in a few weeks.

Paper 4 Listening (approximately 40 minutes)

PART 1

You will hear people talking in eight different situations.
For questions **1–8**, choose the best answer **A, B** or **C**.

1 You are walking down the street when somebody stops you and speaks to you. What does he want you to do?

   A give him directions

   B give him an address

   C take him somewhere

2 You hear someone talking on a public telephone.
Who is she talking to?

   A her employer

   B another employee

   C a doctor

3 You hear part of a radio news report. Where is the reporter?

   A in a conference hall

   B outside a building

   C in a hotel

4 You hear someone on the radio describing her career.
How does she feel?

   A content

   B frustrated

   C jealous

5 You hear part of a radio report. Who is speaking?

   A a policeman

   B a motoring expert

   C a car driver

6 You hear someone talking on the telephone. What is he doing?

   A giving advice

   B expressing disapproval

   C trying to persuade

7 You hear two people discussing the local bus service.
What's their opinion of it?

   A The service is unreliable.

   B The fares are too high.

   C The journeys are very slow.

8 You hear part of an interview with a sportsman.
What is the situation?

   A He has just won a match.

   B He is about to play.

   C He has decided to retire.

PART 2

You will hear part of a radio programme about Gatwick Airport, an airport near London.

For questions **9–18**, complete the sentences.

GATWICK AIRPORT

There are | 9 | businesses operating at the airport.

Carol Bennett works as an | 10 | .

Carol compares the airport with | 11 | .

The young lady had a problem because she | 12 | when her flight landed in Australia.

The young lady didn't have any | 13 | with her when she arrived at Gatwick Airport.

Carol sent the young lady to | 14 | .

The people who watch what happens in the airport are the | 15 | .

They sometimes have to deal with overcrowding in the | 16 | .

Jane Anderson works in the | 17 | department.

She has problems with passengers whenever | 18 | happen.

PART 3

You will hear five different radio advertisements for places where parties can be held.

For questions **19–23**, choose from the list **A–F** what each place states. Use the letters only once. There is one extra letter which you do not need to use.

A There are sometimes reduced prices.

B There is a free room for big groups.

C You should book well in advance.

D It is an easy place to get to.

E Entertainment is sometimes provided.

F The prices given include everything.

Advert 1	19
Advert 2	20
Advert 3	21
Advert 4	22
Advert 5	23

PART 4

You will hear an interview with someone who started a news service called Children's Express.
For questions **24–30**, choose the best answer **A, B** or **C**.

Children's Express

24 The purpose of Children's Express is to encourage children to

   A   think in a more adult way.

   B   consider important matters.

   C   train as journalists.

25 Bob says that the children who work on Children's Express

   A   are carefully chosen.

   B   learn from each other.

   C   get on well together.

26 What success has Children's Express had?

   A   TV programmes have been made about it.

   B   Adults read some of the articles it produces.

   C   It has affected the opinions of some adults.

27 What did the survey in the *Indianapolis Star* show about the page they write?

   A   It is read by a lot of adults.

   B   It is the most popular page in the paper.

   C   It interests adults more than children.

28 Important public figures agree to be interviewed by the children because

   A   Children's Express has a good reputation.

   B   they like the questions children ask.

   C   they want children to like them.

29 When an article is being prepared, the editors

   A   help the reporters in the interviews.

   B   change what the reporters have written.

   C   talk to the reporters about the interviews.

30 What is unique about their type of journalism?

   A   Nothing in their articles is invented.

   B   Everything that is recorded appears in the articles.

   C   It is particularly suitable for children.

Paper 5 Speaking (15 minutes for 2 candidates)

PART 1
(about 4 minutes)

Practise answering these questions.

Where do you come from?
What is X like? What kind of place is X?
Can you say something about what it's like living there?
How long have you lived there?
How long have you been learning English?

PART 2
(about 4 minutes)

Both candidates should look at pictures 1A and 1B on page 120.

The pictures show places where you can go with your family or friends when you have some free time.

Candidate A

Compare and contrast these pictures, saying how you feel about visiting places like these. You have about a minute to do this.

Candidate B

Talk about which of these places you would prefer to visit. You have about 20 seconds to do this.

Both candidates should now look at pictures 1C and 1D on page 120.

The pictures show different places where you can do your shopping.

Candidate B

Compare and contrast these pictures, saying which type of place you prefer to shop in and why. You have about a minute to do this.

Candidate A

Talk about which type of place you prefer. You have about 20 seconds to do this.

PART 3
(about 3 minutes)

Both candidates should look at the set of pictures 1E on page 121.

The pictures show some of the things young children might do during one day. You have agreed to look after two children while their parents go out for the day. One child is two years old and the other is four. Now you have to plan what you are going to do with them.

Talk to each other about this and use the pictures to help you to plan a day of activities with the children. Talk about how long you will spend on each activity.

PART 4
(about 4 minutes)

Now think about these questions. Tell each other what your opinions are.

- Would you like a job that involved working with little children?

- What kind of person do you need to be if you work with young children?

- Do you think young children are happier at home with their mother or at a kindergarten or nursery with other children?

- What is the best age to start school? Why?

- What are the most important things for parents to teach young children?

Test 2

Paper 1 Reading (1 hour 15 minutes)

PART 1

You are going to read a newspaper article about cars in London. For questions **1–6**, choose from the sentences **A–H** which one best summarizes each section of the article (**1–6**). There is one extra sentence which you do not need to use. There is an example at the beginning (**0**).
Mark your answers **on the separate answer sheet**.

A	The number of cars in London has not fallen.
B	Little can be done to improve the traffic situation in London.
C	New developments have prevented improvements in traffic conditions in London.
D	Using a car in London continues to have advantages.
E	Traffic movement in London today is just as bad as it was in the past.
F	Travelling by other means of transport can be unpleasant.
G	There has been a decrease in certain types of traffic in London.
H	Driving in London is getting worse.

London and the car – facing the 21st Century together

0	*H*

Surrounded by other traffic, halted by thickening jams and constant roadworks, under pressure from mounting regulations, rising costs and environmental reformers – there are plenty of reasons why the London motorist could logically be considered a threatened species.

1	

We all know it. Driving in the capital has been getting more problematic for years. There is clear evidence that the increasingly unpleasant driving conditions in the capital are having some effect on car use. The most marked is that commuting to work by car has fallen by a quarter over the last decade, from 200,000 per peak to 150,000, though this has partly been due to job relocation. The number of large commercial vehicles has fallen too and motorcycle and bicycle use has declined, following a period of rapid growth ten years ago.

2	

Any benefit from this has however been offset by a big increase in the numbers of light commercial and service vehicles, and traffic levels on major roads in the capital have been decreasing only by one per cent a year through the 1990s. This benefit in turn has been outweighed by increases in roadworks – one recent count of holes in the road found a 25 per cent increase against a year ago. Clearly the overall situation is no better for the motorist in the capital, despite the fall in recorded traffic volumes, a fact consistently confirmed by Department of Transport surveys.

3	

Speeds, for example, have hardly increased. In central London they are at times around 16 kph, horse-and-cart stuff, with the daytime traffic as heavy as traditional rush-hour flows, but often travelling slower because fewer drivers are on familiar trips. Average speeds on all main roads are around 25 kph in the busiest periods, the sort of speed a fast horse and carriage might have achieved a century ago. It is worth remembering that reports from that period speak of carriages packed so tightly together on London's streets that you could have walked on their roofs from one side of the city to the other.

4	

So is the London motorist in total despair? Not yet. Fewer commuting cars may be coming in, but there are 2.3 million cars registered in the city, and no evidence that numbers are falling. In 1971 half the households in London had cars, with more than 9 per cent having two or more. By 1991 (the last year for official figures) 60 per cent had cars and nearly 18 per cent had two or more. Even in central London, where car-owning conditions are hardly the most attractive, 46 per cent of households had a car and 10 per cent had two or more. So even if the London motorist is using the car a bit less, that car – and increasingly a second car – is still sitting outside.

5	

And for all the problems of driving around and parking in London, the car can still be good news for the traveller. The very latest statistics from the Department of Transport are based on door-to-door travel times for a sample of identical journeys actually made by London residents within the last 12 months. They reveal the following average total times in minutes: by car, 40; by rail/tube, 43; by bus, 58, by bicycle, 37. These calculations took into account the time needed to park and walk, and the time spent by bus and rail/tube travellers waiting for their transport. Nearly three-quarters of the rail/tube journey time was taken up by waiting. Car travellers on the same route spent one third of their time standing still.

6	

The advantages of using a bicycle are self-evident in terms of travel time, and everyone knows that the exercise is beneficial. But few who are not very keen pedallers would not be put off by the dangers of sharing roadspace with other traffic, by the fumes, by the limitations on what can be carried on a bike, and by the fairly regular likelihood of arriving wet and cold.

PART 2

You are going to read a newspaper article. For questions **7–14**, choose the answer (**A, B, C** or **D**) which you think fits best according to the text.
Mark your answers **on the separate answer sheet**.

The interview

'We would like to interview you …'. Joyful words for the job-seeker, but my letter carried a warning: 'You will be required to take a psychometric test.' More than 70 per cent of companies now use these 'objective' tests for potential employees. They are meant to give a true picture of candidates that removes the unfairness that may result from the personal opinions of interviewers.

On the day of my interview for the job of assistant to a company Public Relations consultant, my nerves were made worse by finding that the office was close to a hospital with particularly unhappy associations. Luckily, I had deliberately got there early so that I was able to calm myself down before a secretary rushed me upstairs for my test.

Keeping to a strict time limit, I had to assess groups of adjectives, marking which most and which least matched my ideas of myself at work. Choosing one quality out of four when all seemed appropriate was difficult, more difficult than the interview that followed – though I felt I hadn't impressed in that either.

Confirmation of this arrived a week later. My rejection letter was accompanied by a copy of the Private and Confidential Personal Profile Analysis – two and a half sides of paper, based on that 10-minute test.

The Profile's rude inaccuracy and its judgemental tone were harder to accept than the fact that I had been turned down for the job. Apparently, I have 'no eye for detail'; I am also 'a forceful individual … who leads rather than directs' and am 'motivated by financial reward to pay for good living.' The words 'impatient', 'restless' and 'strong-willed' also came up.

'A portrait of an ambitious, power-mad person,' said a psychologist friend of 15 years to whom I showed the Profile. She said it didn't apply to me at all.

I know myself to be a careful, industrious checker. I am shy but cheerful and a bit over-anxious to be thought creative. I am not a power-crazed person.

What would I do, I worried, if I had to take another test for another job, and this unattractive personality emerged again?

I sent the company a polite disagreement with the Profile, purely for the record. Meanwhile, I made a few enquiries.

Had my emotional state of mind made the results untypical of me? I had been disturbed to find the office so close to a hospital that held unhappy memories for me.

'State of mind will have an impact,' says Shane Pressey, an occupational psychologist, 'but on the whole its effect will be relatively minor. It appears that the test was an inadequate tool for the amount of information they were trying to get out of it, and it is not surprising that there were inaccuracies.'

Too late for that particular job, I arranged to sit another psychometric test. This one took much longer and was more thorough; the profile was also more detailed and accurate – it showed my eye for detail and the fact that I have a problem meeting deadlines.

But a peculiar result is hard to challenge without seeming unable to take criticism. It is simply not acceptable to refuse to take a test, in case the job candidate seems uncooperative and eccentric. The interview, with its yes/no personal feeling, is here to stay, but so is objective testing.

If my experience is anything to go by, the job candidate should be suspicious of 10-minute tests that result in generalised – and possibly wildly inaccurate – judgements. I accept that it would be costly to arrange for face-to-face discussions of test results with all job candidates, but a telephone call would be preferable to simply receiving a written 'profile' through the post and having no opportunity to discuss its contents.

7 Before the writer took the test, she

    A felt that she was unlikely to do it very well.

    B made sure that she was mentally prepared for it.

    C believed that such tests were fair to candidates.

    D did some research into tests of that kind.

8 What did the writer think when she took the test?

    A She could not understand some of the questions.

    B She found that there was not enough time to do it.

    C She felt that she had not done it very well.

    D She decided that it would not prove anything.

9 What does the writer mean by 'judgemental' in the fifth paragraph?

    A critical

    B impatient

    C impersonal

    D thoughtful

10 When the writer received the Personal Profile Analysis, she

    A was offended by the comments made about her answers.

    B was glad that she had not been offered the job.

    C regretted some of the answers she had given in the test.

    D realized that her personality would not have suited the job.

11 Why did the Profile worry her?

    A It made her feel that she had been too self-confident before.

    B It indicated that she might have trouble getting a job in future.

    C It did not show that she was capable of being a creative person.

    D It told her things about herself that she had not noticed before.

12 What did she find out after taking the test for the job?

    A The way she was feeling had badly affected her performance in it.

    B Psychometric tests seldom provide reliable information about people.

    C Many job candidates are unwilling to take psychometric tests.

    D It may have been an unsuitable test for its intended purpose.

13 What does the writer recommend?

    A Candidates should be able to talk about their test results with employers.

    B Employers should pay no attention to the results of psychometric tests.

    C Candidates should not be concerned about taking psychometric tests.

    D Employers should stop asking candidates to take psychometric tests.

14 Why does the writer describe her experience?

    A It is typical of experiences that a great many other people have.

    B It shows that no method of selecting job candidates can ever be fair.

    C It is an example of how difficult it can be for someone to get a job.

    D It illustrates faults in a new method of assessing job candidates.

PART 3

You are going to read a newspaper article about swimming lessons. Seven paragraphs have been removed from the article. Choose from the paragraphs **A–H** the one which fits each gap (**15–20**). There is one extra paragraph which you do not need to use. There is an example at the beginning (**0**).
Mark your answers **on the separate answer sheet**.

In the swim

Saturday morning at the Bloomsbury Pool, London. Ken Martin, a man in his twenties, is getting reacquainted with the deep end.

0	*H*

The years since then suggest otherwise. He grew up to join the 25 per cent of the population of Britain who cannot swim and are afraid of water.

He is a member of the Aquaphobic Swimming Club (ASC), which believes that the only way to get a non-swimmer swimming is through one-to-one tuition. So every non-swimmer joining it gets to work with their own individual instructor.

Right now Ken is practising the crawl, swimming just a short distance and then back again, watched closely by his instructor.

Back in the shallow end, Mick Balfour is joined in the pool by his instructor for his seventeenth lesson. 'My first major breakthrough was deciding to come here at all. I just felt that by now, coming up to 40, swimming is something I ought to be able to do,' he says.

16

'I always used to panic when I got my face under the water and would just grab at the nearest available object, which usually turned out to be my instructor.'

17

'You found them OK, but how many should go down? Two. How many did go down? One.' he is told, with a shake of the head.

The ASC was formed in 1978 by a swimming teacher, Peter Cooper. Originally trained as a schoolteacher, he found his true vocation in sports. He found he had a particular talent for helping children who were nervous of the water. What he did not know was that there were many adults with the same problem.

18

'Shortly after that, I started taking people in groups of four. That proved difficult because of the wide differences in age and ability among the students, so I took it down to pairs, and from there to individual lessons.

'I've had people telling me they couldn't stand putting their face in the shower. They have nightmares about water and some feel ill before they come here.'

19

'Our idea of success is that a student gains the ability to swim in deep water with confidence. I reckon on 75 per cent of members reaching that stage. I consider that to be a very high success rate considering some of the psychological problems involved.'

20

'Partly my problem was to do with a fear of water, but as well as that, I grew up in a fishing family, and very few members of a fishing family can actually swim. It used to be considered bad luck for a fisherman to be able to swim.'

Peter goes off to introduce a new student to his instructor. The student stands in the shallow end, holding on to a float. The instructor grips the other end. The student hesitatingly eases forward and moves around in a circle, grasping the float. After a few circles more, the instructor relaxes his grip until only his fingers rest on the tip. The student is suddenly floating solo. It's a start.

A Today they are working on breathing to sort this particular problem out. 'As you move forward, blow the air out,' his instructor reminds him. 'This will help you relax.' Face down in the water, he pushes himself forward, loses control, and regains his feet.

B 'Don't rush your strokes,' calls his instructor. 'Do that and you'll tire yourself. Then you think you won't make it, so then you worry. Remember, the aim is simply to have you floating in the deep end – relaxed.'

C John Riney, a 39-year-old construction worker, knows about those. He's been coming to the ASC since January. 'I come from the west coast of Ireland, down by the sea, and never learned how to swim,' he explains.

D Courses like theirs consist of eleven 30-minute lessons with a personal instructor. The ASC also has the 'Dolphin Club', which offers similar tuition for children.

E 'But anybody can swim. If you can relax the mind, the body will follow. This isn't something you can get out of a textbook – you have to teach them, you have to know what's going on in the student's mind.'

F 'I was extremely nervous,' he goes on. 'The first hurdle was just getting used to being in the water. For the first eight lessons I just could not get my feet off the floor of the pool.'

G 'I got a telephone call asking me if I did lessons for adults as well. I said no. A week later I got another, and it suddenly occurred to me that there was a demand.'

H The last time he was in deep water he was a child. An all-knowing adult had thrown him in, sure it was the best way of making him swim.

PART 4

You are going to read an article from a magazine called *Bookcase*.
For questions **21–35**, choose from the authors (**A–D**). There is an example at the beginning (**0**).
Mark your answers **on the separate answer sheet**.

Of which author are the following stated?

She wrote a book in which the main character is elderly.	**0** D
She used personal experience in one of her books.	**21**
She wrote a book that didn't seem likely to be interesting.	**22**
She has been a writer for longer than some people may realize.	**23**
She made a prediction about a certain type of book.	**24**
She went through a difficult period in her life.	**25**
She suffered a disaster concerning one of her books.	**26**
She has written about hidden feelings.	**27**
One of her books became successful some time after it was first published.	**28**
She had difficulty in writing one of her books.	**29**
She has written in an amusing way.	**30**
Her books have always dealt with matters of right and wrong.	**31**
Her latest book has been even more popular than her previous ones.	**32**
She has noticed a change in the type of book she writes.	**33**
She has a preference for books that describe everyday events.	**34**
Her latest book is different from her others.	**35**

Encounters with top authors

Over the course of 50 issues, we've been through literally thousands of new fiction titles in an effort to steer our readers in the direction of the best new books and the most promising authors. In fact, several of today's best-loved novelists were featured in *Bookcase* before they reached the top of the bestseller lists. So, to celebrate our 50th anniversary, we look back on some early encounters with today's most popular writers.

A   JILLY COOPER

Prior to 1986, Jilly had published a string of domestic romances, but was still best known for her hilarious articles in *The Sunday Times*. So when all her passion and wicked sense of humour came pouring out in *Riders*, a 900-page tale of ambition on horseback, *Bookcase* invited her to write a background piece for the magazine. Among Jilly's admissions were that the main character, Jake, was based on her own childhood riding teacher, Mr Green; that she'd lost the original 50,000-word manuscript on a bus in 1971; and that, second time around, she'd almost come to a stop after a few chapters. Yet, despite all this, *Riders* ran on to become a number-one bestseller.

B   P.D. JAMES

Certain authors have such a reputation that we are always interested in their work. P.D. James is a case in point – an original writer of crime fiction for more than 30 years. Prior to publishing her acclaimed novel, *A Taste For Death*, she wrote an article for *Bookcase* about the development of the English murder mystery, in which she observed that the gentle puzzles of the past had given way to a darker form reflecting a moral crisis in society. 'The detective story has moved closer to the style of other novels,' she said, 'and this is a trend which will continue.' Her words were put into action. As recently as the last issue of *Bookcase*, we reviewed *The Children of Men*, which marks a major change of direction for P.D. Appealing to her widest audience yet, this is a terrifying, futuristic morality tale.

C   JOANNA TROLLOPE

If you thought Joanna Trollope was a recent success, think again. Her long career as a published author began in 1975. And when *Bookcase* visited her in 1991, she had just had five years of relative financial hardship. *Bookcase's* interest had been aroused by the easily readable, yet thought-provoking style of her third novel, *A Passionate Man*, about emotions beneath the surface of English village life. As it turned out, this book was to light up her slow-burning career. 'Perhaps the public has been fed impersonal fiction for too long,' said Joanna, who herself favours writing with 'an appetite for dealing with life as we really live it.' Today, the appetite for Joanna's work is so strong that even a re-issue of her earlier novel, *The Choir*, reached number one in Britain.

D   ROSAMUNDE PILCHER

It didn't sound that promising: a novel by a 63-year-old grandmother, featuring a heroine her own age; a novel distinctly short on blood, passion and glamour; a novel, instead, about the complexities and pleasures of family life. Yet *Bookcase* was charmed by Rosamunde Pilcher's story-telling and set off to interview her immediately. It emerged that Rosamunde had written 12 published novels prior to *The Shell Seekers*. She had stuck to her beliefs, reasoning that 'people are looking for moral standards.' Her instincts were right. In America, the book hit the *New York Times* bestseller list and stayed there for three months. A star was born.

Paper 2 Writing (1 hour 30 minutes)

PART 1

You **must** answer this question.

1   An Australian friend of your family is coming soon to visit you. Part of a letter from your friend is given below.

Read the letter carefully. Then write a letter answering your friend's question and describing some possible presents for yourself and your family. You should choose at least two of the presents shown in the pictures below.

> Just a note to let you know I'll be arriving on March 14th at 16.00. Is there any chance you'll be able to meet me at the airport? Don't worry if you can't.
>
> By the way, I'd like to bring some presents for you and your family, so please give me a few suggestions. Otherwise, I may choose something you don't like!
>
> See you soon.
>
> Yours,
>
> Jo

Your suggestions for presents:

Write a **letter** of **120–180** words in an appropriate style. Do not write any addresses.

PART 2

Write an answer to **one** of the questions **2–5** in this part. Write your answer in **120–180** words in an appropriate style, putting the question number in the box.

---

2   You want to improve your English by working at an American summer camp for children under the age of 12. At the camp, the children can do a variety of activities connected with sport, music or the arts.

Write a **letter of application** for work, giving details of two or three activities you could help to run.

3   Every year your English teacher organizes a writing competition. This year, these are the instructions:

Write an account of a big public event – for example, a football match or a music festival – which you went to and enjoyed. First prize will be given to the account which best expresses what it was like to be there.

Write your **account** for the competition.

4   An international magazine is asking its readers of all ages for their opinions on this question:

How much should parents control what their children watch on television?

Some of the best articles written by readers will be printed in the magazine.

Write your **article** to send to the magazine, describing your own opinions and experiences.

5   **Background reading texts**

Answer **one** of the following two questions based on your reading of **one** of the set books. Write the title of the book next to the question number box.

5(a)   How does the book which you have read end? Is there anything which you would like to change about the ending?

5(b)   Describe the character you find most interesting in the book which you have read. Explain why you have chosen this character.

Paper 3 Use of English (1 hour 15 minutes)

PART 1

For questions **1–15**, read the text below and decide which word or phrase **A, B, C** or **D** best fits each space. There is an example at the beginning (**0**). Mark your answers **on the separate answer sheet**.

Example:

| **0** | **A** made | **B** become | **C** had | **D** done |

| 0 | A | **B** | C | D |

EYEWITNESS GUIDES

It all started just six years ago with *Birds*. Since then, Eyewitness Guides have (**0**) .... a publishing sensation – 50 subjects (**1**) ...., 40 countries conquered, 15 million copies sold. But the success of Eyewitness Guides cannot be (**2**) .... in statistics alone, (**3**) .... these high-quality reference books have established a (**4**) .... original way of presenting information.

We live in an age of television, video and interactive computing, in which children are (**5**) .... at absorbing data from images at a glance. (**6**) .... this makes them respond favourably to visual learning, the disadvantage is that they sometimes lack confidence with words. So, what the Eyewitness Guides have done is to combine the two elements, words and pictures, (**7**) .... them as just one thing – entertainment.

One of the main reasons (**8**) .... the books' success is the discovery that, against a white background, even the most (**9**) .... objects can look wonderful. Often a single photographic image will take (**10**) .... an entire double-page spread, grabbing your (**11**) .... . Whatever the image, you'll always find the text (**12**) .... alongside, building your understanding of the subject.

Eyewitness Guides are the (**13**) ....of a unique approach, in which photographs, models, maps and diagrams are specially produced. Everything is done to make (**14**) .... that they compete with the impact of television images. But these books have one (**15**) .... advantage – children can return to them again and again, finding something fresh to read every time.

1	**A**	dealt	**B**	fulfilled	**C**	covered	**D**	managed
2	**A**	scored	**B**	valued	**C**	numbered	**D**	measured
3	**A**	for	**B**	out of	**C**	due to	**D**	from
4	**A**	fully	**B**	completely	**C**	considerably	**D**	widely
5	**A**	capable	**B**	powerful	**C**	effective	**D**	skilled
6	**A**	In contrast	**B**	While	**C**	Even so	**D**	Despite
7	**A**	conducting	**B**	treating	**C**	operating	**D**	applying
8	**A**	under	**B**	behind	**C**	beneath	**D**	below
9	**A**	accustomed	**B**	habitual	**C**	repeated	**D**	familiar
10	**A**	up	**B**	in	**C**	to	**D**	on
11	**A**	fascination	**B**	involvement	**C**	attraction	**D**	attention
12	**A**	quite	**B**	nearby	**C**	right	**D**	next
13	**A**	outcome	**B**	production	**C**	formation	**D**	effect
14	**A**	certain	**B**	definite	**C**	firm	**D**	guaranteed
15	**A**	high	**B**	large	**C**	major	**D**	grand

PART 2

For questions **16–30**, read the text below and think of the word which best fits each space. Use only **one** word in each space. There is an example at the beginning **(0)**.
Write your word **on the separate answer sheet**.

Example: | **0** | *them* |

Vegetarianism

Vegetarians don't eat any meat, fish or poultry, and they avoid foods with animal products in **(0)** .... . Some people avoid red meat but they include chicken and fish **(16)** .... their diet. These are often people who recognize **(17)** .... health benefits of a vegetarian diet, but who find they can't **(18)** .... up meat completely. This half-way position is sometimes taken by people who are making the change **(19)** .... a completely vegetarian diet. Vegans go one step further **(20)** .... other vegetarians, avoiding all foods of animal origin, such as dairy produce, eggs and honey.

Vegetarians are growing in number. **(21)** .... estimated seven per cent of British people are now vegetarian, and there are a **(22)** .... many others who only eat meat occasionally. In the **(23)** .... few years, food manufacturers have expanded their vegetarian ranges, and it has **(24)** .... a lot easier to choose an animal-free diet. Many restaurants also now offer a wide variety **(25)** .... vegetarian dishes.

People might choose a vegetarian diet **(26)** .... moral or health reasons, **(27)** .... both. Some vegetarians simply don't like the idea of eating other creatures, and they may dislike the conditions in **(28)** .... many animals are kept before **(29)** .... killed for food. Others may have become vegetarians **(30)** .... of the health benefits.

PART 3

For questions **31–40**, complete the second sentence so that it has a similar meaning to the first sentence. Use the word given and other words to complete each sentence. **You must not use more than five words. Do not change the word given.** There is an example at the beginning (**0**).
Write **only** the missing words **on the separate answer sheet**.

Example:

0 'Do you know how to get to the town centre?' she asked me.

way

She asked me .... to the town centre.

The gap can be filled by the words

0	*whether I knew the way*	OR	**0**	*if I knew the way*

---

31 The authorities have improved the public transport system here recently.

improvements

The authorities .... the public transport system here recently.

32 I was too scared to tell him what I really thought.

courage

I .... to tell him what I really thought.

33 It was easy for us to get tickets for the concert.

no

We .... tickets for the concert.

34 He pretended to be enjoying himself, but he wasn't really.

as

He acted .... himself, but he wasn't really.

35 They probably don't live at the same address any more.

doubt

I .... at the same address any more.

36 I didn't agree with the idea.

favour

I .... the idea.

37 Sandra said that she was willing to work late.

mind

Sandra said that .... late.

38 You're tired because you stayed up very late last night.

if

You wouldn't be tired .... to bed earlier last night.

39 The number of tourists visiting this area rose last year.

rise

Last year .... the number of tourists visiting this area.

40 I hadn't made a speech before, so I was very nervous.

used

Because I .... speeches, I was very nervous.

PART 4

For questions **41–55**, read the text below and look carefully at each line. Some of the lines are correct, and some have a word which should not be there. If a line is correct put a tick (✓) by the number **on the separate answer sheet**. If a line has a word which should **not** be there, write the word **on the separate answer sheet**. There are two examples at the beginning (**0**) and (**00**).

Examples:

0	✓
00	*one*

LONDON

0	London is a big city, but many of the people who live there regard it as
00	a number of small towns put together. Each one district has its own
41	identity and atmosphere and some of parts are even described by their
42	inhabitants as 'villages'. Much of the centre of the city consists of shops
43	and businesses and the majority of people they live in the suburbs. A great
44	many of them travel to work in the city every day by a train, bus, tube or
45	car; this is called commuting. Commuters might spend as much as two
46	hours every morning getting to work and too another two hours getting
47	home again. The cost of living in London is higher than so in most other
48	parts of Britain, and many people are paid extra money on the top of their
49	salaries because of this. Millions of visitors come to London every year
50	from all over the world for to see the famous sights, such as Buckingham
51	Palace, in where the Queen lives, and many other historic buildings. London
52	is also very famous for including its theatres, red buses and black taxis.
53	Some people find it as a noisy, dirty place but it has many large,
54	pleasant parks where everyone can enjoy themselves some peace and
55	quiet. London has many attractions there, both for people from overseas and
	for people from other parts of Britain.

PART 5

For questions **56–65**, read the text below. Use the word given in capitals at the end of each line to form a word that fits in the space in the same line. There is an example at the beginning (**0**).
Write your word **on the separate answer sheet**.

Example: | **0** | *development* |

Road Maps

The (**0**) .... of the road maps of Britain that exist today started   **DEVELOP**

over 200 years ago. The Army was concerned about the (**56**) ....   **POSSIBLE**

of enemy invasion, but its plans for (**57**) .... were hindered by the   **DEFEND**

lack of maps at the time. Those that did exist were (**58**) .... and   **ACCURATE**

lacked detail.

Work to produce (**59**) .... maps was carried out by an organization   **RELY**

called Ordnance Survey. They were remarkably (**60**) .... . Using   **SUCCEED**

fairly simple instruments, they produced (**61**) .... accurate results   **SURPRISE**

and set the high standard for which British maps have a (**62**) .... .   **REPUTE**

Map-makers today use totally different methods. Today's (**63**) ....   **MOTOR**

have a vast (**64**) .... of road atlases produced by a wide range of   **CHOOSE**

publishers. They (**65**) .... enormously in style, colour and content   **VARIOUS**

but they all derive from the maps produced by Ordnance Survey.

Paper 4 Listening (approximately 40 minutes)

PART 1

You will hear people talking in eight different situations.
For questions **1–8**, choose the best answer **A, B** or **C**.

1 You hear someone describing something that happened to her.
How did she feel?

A annoyed

B confused

C disappointed

2 You hear part of a radio play.
Where are the speakers?

A in a taxi

B at an airport

C at home

3 You hear this announcement in a supermarket.
What does the announcer want customers to do?

A leave the building now

B buy a certain product

C use a particular exit

4 You hear two people talking on a railway station platform.
What is the relationship between them?

A They are strangers.

B They are colleagues.

C They are neighbours.

5 You hear someone describing a trip.
What did she do during the trip?

A She spent a lot of money.

B She visited a lot of famous places.

C She met a lot of people.

6 You hear the presenter of a local radio news programme.
Who is he going to interview?

A a member of the public

B a local journalist

C a senior politician

7 You hear someone describing the place where she lives.
What does she think of the place?

A It is dangerous.

B It is strange.

C It is interesting.

8 You hear an announcement about a radio programme.
What kind of programme is it?

A a sports programme

B a holiday programme

C a health programme

PART 2

You will hear part of a local radio programme, in which the presenter gives
details of a competition.
For questions **9–18**, fill in the missing information.

Radio Reporter Competition

Reports must be: **9** [   ] long

Aim of competition: to show the **10** [   ] of

the area

Top prize: tape recorder with **11** [   ]

Other prizes for: most interesting subject

12 [   ]

most imaginative presentation

Main categories: the personalities and activities of the area

important local **13** [   ]

Other category for: entries from schools

Winners can buy: **14** [   ] for the school

Reports can be linked to: **15** [   ] done at school

Best reports: to be broadcast on special programme called

16 [   ]

Tapes must be: of good quality and **17** [   ]

To pick up tapes: write **18** [   ] on envelope

PART 3

You will hear five different radio reports.
For questions **19–23**, choose from the list **A–F** what each reporter is reporting
on. Use the letters only once. There is one extra letter which you do not need to
use.

A a concert

B a parade

C a strike

D a demonstration

E a sports event

F a celebration

Report 1 19 [ ]

Report 2 20 [ ]

Report 3 21 [ ]

Report 4 22 [ ]

Report 5 23 [ ]

PART 4

You will hear part of a radio phone-in programme in which teenagers give advice on relationships between parents and teenagers.

For questions **24–30**, write **Y (YES)** next to those views that are expressed by any of the speakers and **N (NO)** next to those views that are not expressed.

Help around the house

24   It may be necessary to allow a teenager to have an untidy bedroom. | 24 |

25   Most teenagers like their rooms to be untidy. | 25 |

26   When children do jobs in the house, they do them badly. | 26 |

27   Teenagers should be forced to do a lot of jobs around the house. | 27 |

28   Parents should insist that their teenage children help in the house. | 28 |

29   It is good if parents allow teenagers to have untidy bedrooms. | 29 |

30   It is bad for teenagers if they don't have to help in the house. | 30 |

Paper 5 Speaking (15 minutes for 2 candidates)

PART 1
(about 4 minutes)

Practise answering these questions.

How old are you?
Do you have a job? OR Are you at school or college?
What kind of work do you do? OR How many more years will you be at school or college?
Which are or were your favourite subjects at school? OR What are you studying at college?
What are your plans for the future?

PART 2
(about 4 minutes)

Both candidates should look at pictures 2A and 2B on page 122.

The pictures show two sports which a lot of people enjoy watching.

Candidate A

Compare and contrast these pictures, saying how you feel about watching these sports. You have about a minute to do this.

Candidate B

Talk about which of these sports you would prefer to watch. You have about 20 seconds to do this.

Both candidates should now look at pictures 2C and 2D on page 122.

The pictures show people meeting their friends for an evening out together.

Candidate B

Compare and contrast these pictures, saying which kind of place you would prefer to go to with your friends and why. You have about a minute to do this.

Candidate A

Talk about which place you would prefer to go to. You have about 20 seconds to do this.

PART 3
(about 3 minutes)

Both candidates should look at the set of pictures 2E on page 123.

The pictures show some of the special evening courses for young adults which your local college is planning to offer. These courses will be in practical subjects which are useful for everyday life.

Talk to each other about this and decide which of these courses you think the college should definitely offer. If only four courses can be run, which two do you think the college should cancel?

PART 4
(about 4 minutes)

Now think about these questions. Tell each other what your opinions are.

- Are there any other useful skills that you think the college should run courses in?

- Do you have any practical skills which are particularly useful or which you enjoy doing?

- What are the most popular leisure interests among your friends?

- How do you relax after a hard day working or studying?

- What do you do to keep yourself fit and healthy?

Test 3

PART 1

You are going to read a leaflet issued by the Post Office in Britain. Choose the most suitable heading from the list **A–I** for each part (**1–7**) of the article. There is one extra heading which you do not need to use. There is an example at the beginning (**0**).

Mark your answers **on the separate answer sheet**.

A	Treating you as an individual
B	Prompt response if you have any problems
C	We're getting fewer complaints than ever before
D	No organisation has all the answers
E	If we don't have it, we'll make sure you get it
F	Nobody wants to be kept hanging around
G	Professionals to deal with you efficiently
H	More reliable self-service facilities
I	The idea behind this

The Post Office Customer Charter

0 *I*

We want to let you know what our service aims are and we want you to let us know where you feel we're succeeding or falling short. We aim to serve you better and we aim to meet high standards in terms of quick service, machines, personal service, professional service, giving information, and dealing with complaints.

1

So, with the help of regular research, we have made it our business to ask you, the customer, exactly what you want from your post office. As you may have already noticed, there is now a poster which gives you the latest information on waiting times at this post office. We also plan to keep you up to date on our performance in other important areas of activity.

At the back you'll find a reply paid card which we hope you'll use to let us have your comments and ideas. The more we hear from you, the better we can serve your needs. And for the 28 million of you who use your local post office every week, that can only be good news.

2

Hardly surprisingly, then, we have set ourselves the key target of reducing waiting times. Exactly how, though?

We carried out detailed surveys to establish when different post offices are busiest, so as to provide the right level of staffing cover. In some post offices, for example, there are very high peaks on Thursday mornings. In others, the greatest demand may be at lunchtimes, or at the end of the month.

To provide better cover at busy times, many extra part-time staff have been recruited, allowing us to schedule more flexibly. In some offices, extra serving positions are provided to meet peak-time demand. Other initiatives include single queues, special service positions and improved stamp vending machines.

3

For customers who simply want to buy a few stamps at their local post office, vending machines can prove a great help. Recognising their speed of service and convenience, we have already invested £1.5 million in new style electronic vending machines that accept all UK coins and give change. Many post offices now have single stamp vending machines internally as well as stamp book machines externally. We regularly check customer requirements, and will continue to extend and improve this network of vending machines wherever possible.

4

Like most other companies handling cash, we normally deal with you from behind a glass screen, which can make it harder to provide you with a personal service. We do our best, however, to overcome this barrier by treating you with courtesy. All our staff are trained in customer care; in fact independent research shows that in more than nine cases out of ten, customers felt that our staff were 'friendly and approachable' and that, even if they were unable to answer a question, they were willing to find somebody who could.

To make our service more personal, our staff will now wear name badges so that you know exactly who you are dealing with. We will also make sure we do the little things – like greeting you and thanking you – that make you feel welcome and valued as a customer.

5

Your local post office has more than 150 products and services available to you. Some of these are straightforward, but others are complex and require in each case different knowledge and expertise on the part of our staff. What's more, nothing stands still. New product and service information constantly needs to be absorbed and kept up to date so that, whenever you ask, your questions can be answered knowledgeably.

The key of course is training, to which we are fully committed. All our staff undergo weekly training – and where possible we can hold these sessions outside opening hours so that service to customers is not reduced.

6

From TV licences to pensions and National Savings certificates. These are just some of the many and varied services we offer.

We will do our best to ensure that the many forms and leaflets associated with all of these are always readily available. If, however, this isn't possible and you can't find what you are looking for, please talk to one of our staff, who will arrange for it to be posted on to you without charge.

7

We'll do our best to sort these out in the shortest time possible. Most of the time, your Branch Manager will be able to sort them out on the spot. If he or she is unable to, or you'd rather put it in writing, we have special Customer Services Units to deal with such queries. Alternatively, you may find it helpful to refer to our Code of Practice (a leaflet is available at this post office).

Our Customer Services Units will acknowledge your letter on the day it is received, and will send a reply no more than seven working days later. In other words, you can normally expect a reply within about ten days of writing.

PART 2

You are going to read a magazine article. For questions **8–15**, choose the answer (**A, B, C** or **D**) which you think fits best according to the text. Mark your answers **on the separate answer sheet**.

Want to write a bestseller?

It's the sort of thing that usually only happens in fiction. A young bank worker buys a home computer and to fill his spare time writes a first novel. A few months later the book has been sold here and abroad in deals worth £750,000; a Hollywood film is under consideration. That, though, has been the experience of Michael Ridpath, who before tapping out *Free to Trade*, a fast-moving thriller about international financial crime, had never written anything more imaginative than a financial report.

For those of us who still haven't found a legal, decent and honest way of getting rich, such stories get us excited. But the trouble with trying to pen a small literary masterpiece is that everyone else is too. Writing unsaleable bestsellers is one of the most popular hobbies in Britain. According to one estimate, 20,000–30,000 manuscripts of proposed books are lying in British publishers' in-trays at any one time. That suggests there must be several hundred thousand people out there nightly peering into word processor screens and seeking inspiration. Blake Friedmann, Mr Ridpath's literary agent, receives 20 to 30 manuscripts a day sent in by hopeful writers, but the company has only seen two writers published from this so-called 'slush pile' in the last decade. Any other London literary agent or publisher will tell you the chances are the same. The sad truth is that for 99.9 per cent of authors, all their masterworks will ever earn is a string of rejection letters, and some praise from Auntie Doris if she can be persuaded to read the thing.

David O'Leary, a literary agent who is currently wading through a huge pile of manuscripts from hopefuls, says: 'The Mr Ridpaths of this world are a bad example. People read about them and think they can do it. But there is a mystery at the heart of writing. The more you see, the more you realise this is the sad truth. Pick up a page and you can tell whether someone can write or not. Some publishers who shall be nameless have a 10-page test. If the story hasn't gripped them by then, they don't read any more.'

Pierre Reylan, one of the readers employed to go through the vast number of unsolicited manuscripts at one publisher, says that the only manuscript sent in unrequested he can remember being published was a non-fiction book – on how to improve your eyesight. 'What impresses me is the huge amount of work and effort going into the manuscripts. It feels sad always having to send them back.' Sometimes a letter will accompany a no-hope manuscript, announcing that the author has given up a perfectly respectable job to spend their whole time writing.

Darley Anderson, a London agent who receives 100 manuscripts a week (he might get up to four writers a year published) insists the talent is out there. 'It's just that some publishers are too lazy, too busy or don't have the imagination to find them.' Two years ago he sold a novel by a nurse, Martina Cole, for £150,000. 'If in that year I had not taken on anybody else I would have felt it was a very successful year.'

The odds against success, then, are enormous. But for some writers the urge to write a book is too great to be resisted, whether it is because of the need for money, the desire to be famous or the wish to be creative.

8   What is unusual about Michael Ridpath?

   A   He has succeeded with his first attempt at writing.
   B   He has written a book set in the financial world.
   C   He has had great success with a non-fiction book.
   D   He has had success as a writer at an early age.

9   What is the 'slush pile', mentioned in the second paragraph?

   A   manuscripts that have been rejected
   B   manuscripts not requested by publishers
   C   manuscripts sent to publishers on one day
   D   manuscripts that are unlikely to be read

10   What is emphasized in the second paragraph?

   A   the low quality of most manuscripts sent to publishers
   B   the effort that is required in order to write a book
   C   the unwillingness of publishers to read manuscripts
   D   the number of people trying to be published authors

11   According to David O'Leary, Michael Ridpath's success has

   A   led other writers to copy the style of his book.
   B   encouraged people who are not good writers.
   C   suggested that publishers' methods do not work.
   D   affected publishers' reactions to manuscripts they receive.

12   What does Pierre Reylan say about the manuscripts he receives?

   A   The people who send them deserve sympathy.
   B   They are usually longer than they should be.
   C   Non-fiction ones have a good chance of success.
   D   He has difficulty deciding which ones to reject.

13   What do some letters accompanying manuscripts indicate?

   A   how little writers understand the system
   B   the difficult circumstances some writers are in
   C   the previous successes some writers have had
   D   how serious the writers are about writing

14   What does Darley Anderson say about the manuscripts he receives?

   A   Too many people who can't write well send them in.
   B   Any of them may come from a possibly successful writer.
   C   It is relatively easy for him to get one published.
   D   Most years none of them are good enough to be published.

15   What is the purpose of the article?

   A   to discourage people from trying to write bestsellers
   B   to emphasize how difficult it is to write a good book
   C   to describe some of the difficulties that publishers face
   D   to point out how hard it is to get a book published

PART 3

You are going to read part of a careers leaflet about working with animals. Seven sentences have been removed from the passage. Choose from the sentences **A–H** the one which fits each gap (**16–21**). There is one extra sentence which you do not need to use. There is an example at the beginning (**0**).

Mark your answers **on the separate answer sheet**.

SAFARI PARK KEEPER

Annie Stewart has been a keeper at Woburn Animal Kingdom for the past twelve years, and for eight years before that worked at Longleat Safari Park. It's hard physical work, out in all weathers – animals have to be fed and looked after every day of the year.

'My working day normally begins at 8 am, but if an animal's sick I may have to be up all night with it. **0** *H*

It's a five-day week, on a rota, including weekends and bank holidays. They're obviously our busiest times while we're open to visitors between March and October. I begin by loading feeds onto the Land Rover, then I drive to the eland (a type of larger antelope). I feed and check them, making sure none are injured or sick and that they have plenty of hay in their shed. **16** In the winter we have to be careful not to let the animals out too early when the weather is cold, particularly if they are young.

We always have to take special care in our dealings with the rhino – remember that they are dangerous wild animals. **17** And the eland can be especially unpredictable when strangers are around. They only trust two of us to go near them, so if there are any problems with them on my day off I might easily be called in.

During the season when we're open to the public, it's part of the keepers' job to patrol the park in Land Rovers, watching the public as much as the animals.

People can be amazingly silly, ignoring signs and warnings. **18** Some get out of their cars to take photographs when they're frighteningly close to an animal that could kill them in an instant. It's not uncommon for people to stop and picnic; last year some people were found picnicking amongst the tigers! We have to try and be diplomatic and maintain a sense of humour, especially on days when there are queues of traffic and everyone's getting short-tempered. The keepers maintain radio contact all the time, so if there is any problem with either the public or the wildlife, help is never far away.

19 I'm responsible for some 70 of them, each of which has a name. I fill in a daily diary and a weekly report, making a note of any changes of behaviour.

This is a job which requires dedication and hard work. **20** I'd had experience of looking after dogs in boarding kennels, and I was fascinated by the safari park concept. So I wrote to them and was lucky enough to get a job, learning as I went along.

Chipperfields, who part own Longleat and Woburn, were at that time opening up safari parks around the world. I found myself travelling to Uganda on a catching trip and to Spain, Germany and Japan to open parks, as well as to Malaysia and Thailand, transporting animals. **21** It's like a wild animal farm here – the animals have plenty of freedom and I enjoy the independence and responsibility which are central to my job'.

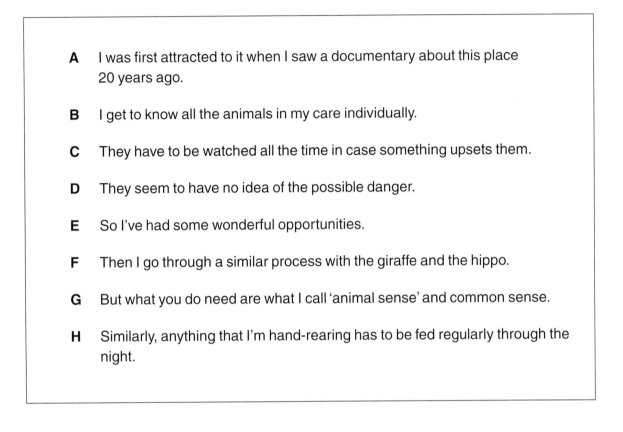

A I was first attracted to it when I saw a documentary about this place 20 years ago.

B I get to know all the animals in my care individually.

C They have to be watched all the time in case something upsets them.

D They seem to have no idea of the possible danger.

E So I've had some wonderful opportunities.

F Then I go through a similar process with the giraffe and the hippo.

G But what you do need are what I call 'animal sense' and common sense.

H Similarly, anything that I'm hand-rearing has to be fed regularly through the night.

PART 4

You are going to read a newspaper article in which various people talk about different electronic personal organisers.

For questions **22–35**, choose from the personal organisers (**A–E**). When more than one answer is required, these may be given in any order. There is an example at the beginning (**0**).

Mark your answers **on the separate answer sheet**.

Of which of the personal organisers A–E do the testers state the following?

It has confusing instructions.	0	*B*
It is not the same kind of machine as the others.	22	
It lacks two important features.	23	
It has a special feature that is not very useful.	24	
Its size is a result of the large number of features it has.	25	
It makes an awful sound.	26	
It contains something I found rather difficult to understand.	27	
It is only good for a certain type of person.	28	
It can be used with other types of machine.	29	
One part of it is too small.	30	
You can find out how to use it without reading an instruction book.	31	
It would help me with a problem I have.	32	33
It is better than what I currently use.	34	
It provides more than just information.	35	

Personal Facts

If you're fed up with bits of paper falling out of notebooks, it might be time to invest in an electronic personal organiser. We got a group of non-experts to test a selection:

A   Special Feature: Handwriting recognition

TESTER: Nikki, designer, 28

'This is very user-friendly and the manual is written in easy to understand steps. There aren't many on-screen instructions, but it's simple to master the use with repetition. The 'to do' list is the best feature – when the machine is switched on it tells you to turn to your diary, handy for us absent-minded ones. The built-in calculator is useful too.

The concept of an organiser that accepts handwriting is good, but in practice it is too time-consuming and impractical. It's simpler just to write things down and be done with it.

It's easy to carry as it's the same size as a thick notebook. However, it's a very expensive way to store basic information.'

B   Special Feature: Anniversary Listing

TESTER: Alison, singer, 24

'This isn't very easy to use, the instruction book isn't clear and a lot of the function keys are difficult to see. It has only five functions – telephone and anniversary listings, a calculator, schedule and clock – a 'to do' facility and a dictionary would be useful. The small screen means you can only display four lines of information at any time.

It's very light and compact, it fits in a jacket pocket, but really it's 'user-unfriendly' and designed only for people who are obsessed with gadgets.'

C   Special Feature: Expenses

TESTER: Andy, DJ, 29

'This was fairly easy to use, it took only about 15 minutes trying it out until I'd worked it out. It's good for my line of work, as it can store loads of personal and work addresses and phone numbers, plus there's a memo schedule feature – great for me as I'm always forgetting things – and a calendar which was handy. It was also very easy to carry – pocket size and light, and it is much more convenient than my notebook. The expenses feature was quite useful but a little complex. The organiser also had an annoying bleep and I couldn't work out how to switch it off! If I was buying one, then I would seriously consider this model.'

D   Special Feature: Spell check and thesaurus

TESTER: Paula, saleswoman, 25

'Although this isn't a personal organiser as such, I did find it useful for the spell check and thesaurus. It's very easy to use, with an adequate instruction book.

It's cassette sized, so very handy to carry around. Obviously, it couldn't replace my current system, but it is very good for the features it does have. It also has a crossword and hangman game, which is really entertaining.'

E   Special Feature: Built-in word processor and thesaurus

TESTER: Andrea, journalist, 23

'This is a very comprehensive option if you're looking for an organiser to use for a wide variety of tasks. There are two instruction manuals, but they're very clear and you can just refer to them as you go along.

The built-in word processor that connects to personal computers is a very attractive asset, and will appeal to anyone on the move in their job. It's larger and heavier than some organisers, but that's to be expected when you consider its functions, and it's still a reasonably convenient size.

I've never thought of buying an organiser before, but if I did, this is certainly an attractive model.'

Paper 2 Writing (1 hour 30 minutes)

PART 1

You **must** answer this question.

1   You have received a letter from your English pen friend, who has recently started at college and is having some problems. You want to find out more about these problems and offer some advice.

Read carefully the extract from the letter below, the notes you have written on it and your list of suggestions. Then write a letter in which you ask for more information about your friend's problems and offer some advice, using the list of suggestions to give you some ideas.

I've just finished my first term at college, and I'm surprised at how hard it has been. There is so much to do. I feel exhausted, and I find it difficult to hand in my work on time. It's quite noisy where I live, so it's hard to study. And I've got no money! It all makes me feel like giving up!

Work or social life?

Eating/ sleeping well?

Can you move?

No, don't!

SUGGESTIONS:

Talk to teachers
Study in college library
Plan time better
Get holiday job

Write a **letter** of **120–180** words in an appropriate style. Do not write any addresses.

PART 2

Write an answer to **one** of the questions **2–5** in this part. Write your answer in **120–180** words in an appropriate style, putting the question number in the box.

---

2   Your English teacher wants to show your class a video and has asked you to suggest a suitable film. It must be a film which everyone will enjoy and it must give the class some good practice in understanding English.

Write a **report** for your teacher, describing the film you want to suggest and saying why you have chosen it.

3   A magazine for learners of English is organizing a short story competition. You have to write a story which begins with the words:

Starting something new is never easy, and Jan woke up that morning feeling very nervous.

Write your **story** for the competition.

4   Your local tourist office has summer jobs available in your area for tour guides to work with groups of English-speaking visitors. Most of these tourists will be retired people in their sixties or seventies.

Write a **letter of application**, saying why you think you are a suitable person to do this job and mentioning one or two places you would take these tourists to.

5   **Background reading texts**

Answer **one** of the following two questions based on your reading of **one** of the set books. Write the title of the book next to the question number box.

5(a)   Which female character do you like best in the book which you have read? Describe the character and say what her importance is to the story.

5(b)   Does the book which you have read have anything special to teach its readers? What ideas do you think the author is trying to express? Write a **report** for your class, covering both of these questions.

Paper 3 Use of English (1 hour 15 minutes)

PART 1

For questions **1–15**, read the text below and decide which word or phrase **A, B, C** or **D** best fits each space. There is an example at the beginning (**0**). Mark your answers on the **separate answer sheet**.

Example:

| 0 | **A** special | **B** one | **C** individual | **D** alone |

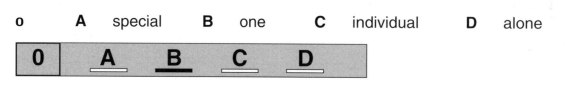

Bowls

If you can roll a ball, you can play bowls. Everyone can play: young and old, men and women, the fit and the not so fit. It is the **(0)** .... outdoor game that **(1)** .... is a sport for all. What other sport can grandparents play on **(2)** .... terms with their grandchildren? What other game is so simple that you could take it up today and be **(3)** .... in the national championships tomorrow?

Simple? Perhaps that's not the **(4)** .... word. There are bowls players in their thousands who will tell you that, although bowls is a game that anyone can **(5)** .... in five minutes, it takes a lifetime to **(6)** .... it. They are the people who have **(7)** .... a passionate interest in the game. **(8)** ...., for outsiders, bowls is another world, and a strange and puzzling one. They see a bowls game in **(9)** .... and wonder what is going on.

What the players are trying to do is easy to explain. Their **(10)** .... is to roll their bowls, called woods, as near as possible to the little white ball, called the jack. If one of your bowls finishes nearer to the jack than your **(11)** ...., you score one point and he or she scores nothing. If you have the two nearest, you score two, and **(12)** .... . The skill **(13)** .... in rolling a bowl that weighs around 2 kilos across about 40 metres so that it stops only a very short **(14)** .... from the target is just as **(15)** .... as the skills required in other sports.

1	**A** exactly	**B** really	**C** precisely	**D** accurately
2	**A** alike	**B** equal	**C** parallel	**D** matching
3	**A** competing	**B** entering	**C** getting	**D** going
4	**A** right	**B** suitable	**C** genuine	**D** just
5	**A** catch on	**B** see through	**C** find out	**D** pick up
6	**A** manage	**B** tame	**C** master	**D** control
7	**A** assembled	**B** produced	**C** developed	**D** grown
8	**A** Besides	**B** Unlike	**C** However	**D** Although
9	**A** performance	**B** movement	**C** practice	**D** action
10	**A** point	**B** attempt	**C** scheme	**D** aim
11	**A** competitor's	**B** opponent's	**C** contestant's	**D** opposer's
12	**A** further	**B** so on	**C** moreover	**D** as follows
13	**A** involved	**B** connected	**C** relating	**D** belonging
14	**A** distance	**B** extent	**C** range	**D** length
15	**A** respectable	**B** impressive	**C** appreciative	**D** favourable

PART 2

For questions **16–30**, read the text below and think of the word which best fits each space. Use only **one** word in each space. There is an example at the beginning (**0**).
Write your word **on the separate answer sheet**.

Example: | **0** | *of* |

The Trinidad Carnival

Festivals in the Caribbean can be huge, colourful events that stretch the imagination. One of the biggest (**0**) .... these, the Trinidad Carnival, consists of five days of non-stop parties and music competitions that end (**16**) .... a costumed parade through the streets of the capital, Port of Spain.

The music at the carnival is calypso. Calypso is (**17**) .... than just music for singing and dancing. An evening in a 'calypso tent' will give you a course in Trinidadian politics and (**18**) .... you know all about the island gossip. But (**19**) .... the topic of the songs, calypso's main function is (**20**) .... entertain.

One of the most important parts of the carnival is the calypso competition. This is divided (**21**) .... two sections. First of all, on the Sunday, the best song is judged. Ten finalists each sing two songs in front of (**22**) .... crowd of 30,000. The singers all do (**23**) .... best to give performances that will have the crowd shouting and screaming (**24**) .... more, and the winner receives the highly-prized title of Calypso Monarch.

Then, on the Monday, there is the Roadmarch competition, (**25**) .... the best dance tune is decided. Dancers in fantastic costumes spill out onto the streets (**26**) .... their thousands at 4am and dance in a parade with the calypso bands. This goes on (**27**) .... the carnival ends the following night. The winner is the person (**28**) .... tune is being played most often as the bands pass the place where the judges (**29**) .... situated.

And the music has to be good, to keep as (**30**) .... as half a million people dancing non-stop for five days.

PART 3

For questions **31–40**, complete the second sentence so that it has a similar meaning to the first sentence. Use the word given and other words to complete each sentence. **You must not use more than five words**. **Do not change the word given**. There is an example at the beginning (**0**).
Write **only** the missing words **on the separate answer sheet**.

Example:

0 'Do you know how to get to the town centre?' she asked me.

way

She asked me .... to the town centre.

The gap can be filled by the words

| **0** | *whether I knew the way* | OR | **0** | *if I knew the way* |

---

31 I suppose it's possible that she didn't understand my message.

may

I suppose .... my message.

32 A local mechanic repaired our car.

repaired

We .... by a local mechanic.

33 'Why don't you relax for a while?' she said to me.

take

She suggested .... easy for a while.

34 The information I got from the assistant was so confusing that I didn't know what to do.

such

The assistant .... that I didn't know what to do.

35 'It's not worth worrying about the past,' I told him.

point

I told him that there was .... about the past.

36 If you don't mind, I'd prefer not to sit next to the door.

rather

If you don't mind, ... next to the door.

37 When I left she said that she hoped I had a pleasant journey.

wished

She .... when I left.

38 I offered to help her but she said 'No, thanks.'

turned

She .... of help.

39 I usually walk to work but today I drove.

instead

I drove to work today .... foot.

40 He referred to his notes before answering the question.

look

He .... his notes before answering the question.

PART 4

For questions **41–55**, read the text below and look carefully at each line. Some of the lines are correct, and some have a word which should not be there. If a line is correct put a tick (✓) by the number **on the separate answer sheet**. If a line has a word which should **not** be there, write the word **on the separate answer sheet**. There are two examples at the beginning (**0**) and (**00**).

Examples:

0	*the*
00	✓

THE INTERVIEW

0	Suzanne was very nervous about her interview. For at the least three
00	weeks before it she was worried about it. She really wanted the job but
41	she knew that a lot of other people wanted get it too. She had been told
42	when she phoned the number in the advert that there were a great many
43	applicants for it, so as she prepared herself. She made notes of what she
44	might be asked and of what she wanted to ask. When the day it came, she
45	arrived half of an hour early. There were six other people waiting to be
46	interviewed. They all looked much more confident than did her. She began
47	to feel herself even more nervous. One by one the others were called.
48	Each of them came out and looking satisfied. Suzanne was the last one to
49	be called into the interview room. She had decided by then time that she
50	had no chance of getting the job, so she felt relaxed as she walked in; she
51	felt that she had nothing to lose. The three interviewers were all them very
52	serious and they didn't seem to be interested in her. She forgot all the
53	answers she had yet prepared and said the first things that came into her
54	head. Afterwards she was sure she wouldn't get the job, but two days
55	later she got a letter for telling her she had been chosen because she had
	been the only one who had acted naturally.

PART 5

For questions **56–65**, read the text below. Use the word given in capitals at the end of each line to form a word that fits in the space in the same line. There is an example at the beginning (**0**).
Write your word **on the separate answer sheet**.

Example: | **0** | *reaction* |

Snow White and the Seven Dwarfs

Public (**0**) .... to the Disney film *Snow White and the Seven Dwarfs*	**REACT**
when it was first shown in 1937 was (**56**) .... . It was received with	**ORDINARY**
great (**57**) .... and it immediately became enormously popular	**EXCITE**
(**58**) .... the world. Good advertising was not the only reason for	**THROUGH**
this (**59**) .... popularity; the film and its characters captured the	**WORLD**
(**60**) .... of people all over the world like no film before it.	**IMAGINE**
In Britain, there were (**61**) .... newspaper articles about the film and	**DAY**
how it was made. *Snow White* toys and books were on (**62**)	**SELL**
everywhere. Some people thought that it might be (**63**) .... for	**UPSET**
children but most people saw it as (**64**) .... entertainment.	**HARM**
Since 1937, it has been re-issued every few years, giving (**65**) .... to	**ENJOY**
many generations of children.	

Paper 4 Listening (approximately 40 minutes)

PART 1

You will hear people talking in eight different situations.
For questions **1–8**, choose the best answer, **A, B** or **C**.

1 You hear a critic describing a film.
What is his opinion of it?

   A   It is dull.

   B   It will shock.

   C   It is peculiar.

2 You hear someone talking on a radio phone-in programme. Where is he phoning from?

   A   his home

   B   his car

   C   his place of work

3 You hear part of a radio play. What is the relationship between the speakers?

   A   They went to the same school.

   B   They have met once before.

   C   They are married to each other.

4 You hear an advertisement on the radio.
What is being advertised?

   A   a special offer

   B   new products

   C   a new shop

5 You are in an airport when someone comes and speaks to you.
What does he want you to do?

   A   show him where Gate 12 is

   B   get some information for him

   C   explain what he should do

6 You hear someone being interviewed on the radio. Who is the speaker?

   A   a composer

   B   an actor

   C   a film director

7 You hear someone talking on the telephone.
What is she doing?

   A   expressing regret

   B   defending herself

   C   offering to do something

8 You hear the presenters of a radio programme talking. What are they going to do?

   A   find out about a city

   B   compare different cities

   C   visit a market

PART 2

You will hear part of a travel programme, in which a reporter talks about various ferries.
For questions **9–18**, fill in the missing information.

FERRIES

FERRY	GOOD POINT	BAD POINT
SEA MASTER	*friendly, competent staff*	9
MAID OF THE OCEAN	10	11
EUROPA	12	*rather dirty*
SEA BREEZE	13	14
WESTERN PRIDE	15	16
BLUE LAGOON	17	18

PART 3

You will hear five different people talking about a famous entertainer.
For questions **19–23**, choose which of the opinions **A–F** each speaker
expresses. Use the letters only once. There is one extra letter which you do not
need to use.

A He isn't very happy.

B He behaves badly.   Speaker 1 | 19 |

Speaker 2 | 20 |

C He is a shy person.

Speaker 3 | 21 |

D He won't be famous for long.

Speaker 4 | 22 |

E He isn't very talented.   Speaker 5 | 23 |

F He is an insincere person

PART 4

You will hear part of an interview with a man who has spent some time living on a desert island.

For questions **24–30**, choose the best answer, **A, B** or **C**.

Island of Dreams

24 What do we learn about Tony at the start of the interview?

   A   His book has become popular.

   B   He has been criticized.

   C   He has had some bad experiences.

25 What made him go to the island?

   A   the desire to write a book about it

   B   dissatisfaction with life in Britain

   C   a book by someone who had been there

26 When Tony and Kathy first went to the island, they

   A   were not equipped for living there.

   B   had to be collected by divers.

   C   were determined not to give up.

27 One reason why they left the island was that

   A   they had not intended to stay forever.

   B   they had achieved what they wanted to.

   C   he thought he could get a better job in Britain.

28 When the storm came, he

   A   had been expecting it.

   B   tied his daughter to the tree.

   C   was frightened by it.

29 What have his experiences on the island taught him?

   A   Life doesn't have to be hard.

   B   Anyone can change their life.

   C   Money doesn't make you happy.

30 The next time Tony goes to the island,

   A   he intends to stay there permanently.

   B   his children may decide not to go with him.

   C   he will act according to his children's wishes.

Paper 5 Speaking (15 minutes for 2 candidates)

PART 1

(about 4 minutes)

Practise answering these questions.

Can you say something about your family?
Do you have any brothers or sisters?
Are they older or younger than you?
Which languages can you speak?
Which language do you speak at home?

PART 2

(about 4 minutes)

Both candidates should look at pictures 3A and 3B on page 124.

The pictures show different ways of spending some time by yourself.

Candidate A

Compare and contrast these pictures, saying how you feel about these activities. You have about a minute to do this.

Candidate B

Talk about which of these things you prefer doing. You have about 20 seconds to do this.

Both candidates should now look at pictures 3C and 3D on page 124.

The pictures show different ways of travelling.

Candidate B

Compare and contrast these pictures, saying which way of travelling you would prefer if you had a long journey to make, and why. You have about a minute to do this.

Candidate A

Talk about which of these ways of travelling you would prefer. You have about 20 seconds to do this.

PART 3

(about 3 minutes)

Both candidates should look at picture 3E on page 125.

The picture is the plan of a flat which two students are going to share. There is a kitchen, a bathroom, one large room and one smaller room.

Talk to each other about this and decide how the two students should arrange the rooms between them. They need somewhere quiet to study and sleep and somewhere they can play music or watch television. Talk about what furniture they need to put in the two rooms. The kitchen and bathroom have everything in them already.

PART 4

(about 4 minutes)

Now think about these questions. Tell each other what your opinions are.

- Do you think it is easier to study in a library or at home?

- What do you think are the good and bad things about being a student?

- Is there any subject that you have never studied, that you would really like to learn about?

- Do you think people can study at any age, or is there a best age for studying?

- In today's world, which subjects are the most important ones for everyone to study? Why?

Test 4

Paper 1 Reading (1 hour 15 minutes)

PART 1

You are going to read a magazine article about noise. Choose from the list **A–I** the sentence that best summarizes each part (**1–7**) of the article. There is one extra sentence which you do not need to use. There is an example at the beginning (**0**).
Mark your answers **on the separate answer sheet**.

A	Noise problems may not be anybody's fault.
B	Many British people suffer in silence.
C	People react differently to noise problems.
D	People like to blame individuals for noise.
E	Noise does not cause as much trouble as people think.
F	A lot of British people complain about noise.
G	There is a new way of dealing with noise problems.
H	Not many noise problems are solved by official action.
I	Noise can cause aggressive behaviour.

Is noise driving you mad?

 I

Summertime in Britain, and for some, life is far from easy. Neighbours open their windows and share their musical tastes with the world or hold noisy outdoor parties, while thumping drills and roaring lorries announce the arrival of summer roadworks. It's enough to drive normally quiet, polite citizens mad. One London market trader attacked a fellow stallholder after seven months of continuous disco music. And an angry neighbour poured weedkiller onto his local golf course after he'd had an earful of early morning tractors and lawnmowers.

But what is it about noise that brings about such extreme reactions? Are the British, as a nation, simply less tolerant of each other, including other people's noise? According to a recent survey, one in three people said their home life was being spoilt by noise from traffic, neighbours, aircraft and trains. Over 84,000 people made a formal complaint about noise last year, according to the Institute of Environmental Health Officers (IEHO); but in well over half of these the complaint was not upheld. 'Noises are often not as loud as the person thinks,' says John Jackson of the IEHO. Also, many complaints are to do with differences in taste rather than volume.

2

This is at the heart of the issue of noise pollution. What irritates one person may be acceptable to another. Officially, over half of British people are living in homes that expose them to noise levels in excess of World Health Organisation recommendations – 55dB, which is quieter than the sound of a phone ringing two metres away. Clearly most of us find this tolerable, or local authorities would be flooded with complaints. But why is noise such a personal thing? Environmental psychologist Dr Jonathan Sime says you often have to look for other reasons why noise is disturbing someone. 'It depends on the time, amount and type of noise and the person – how much they like their privacy, and their general habits.'

3

'Many British people see their home as a private place and want to keep control over it. If noise travels over

these boundaries, it causes annoyance which can lead to stress. Noise from neighbours is probably the most stressful because you can identify the source, and get annoyed with someone in particular – unlike with traffic.' This accords with the league table of noise complaints, which puts neighbours' noise, especially people's voices, radio/TV/hi-fi and pets at the top.

4

If you feel that you have a genuine grievance, British law is of limited help. Part of the problem with making a noise complaint is that there is no fixed level of noise which constitutes a legal nuisance. Most people call the police but they have no powers to intervene. Surprisingly few people contact their local environmental health officer, who has the power to serve a noise-abatement notice saying how the noise must be reduced. Nearly all complaints are remedied informally but if not, the environmental health officer can take offenders to court, where they can be fined. Most cases that get to court result in a fine.

5

One thing to blame in the noise battle is the lack of sound insulation in modern homes and flats, which has worsened the situation. Few properties in Britain are sound-tested after construction or conversion. It may not be that a neighbour is being unreasonably noisy, just that the walls between the two properties are too thin.

6

For most British people, complaining isn't something that we're very good at. The British don't like to make a fuss. People who complain may be described as over-sensitive, and nobody likes to be told what to do in their own home. Seventy per cent of people who object to neighbours' noise take no action at all.

7

There are some bright spots, though. Mediation is becoming popular in noise problems. With a neutral person acting as referee to help find a solution to the problem, many a noise dispute has been resolved. Unlike making an official complaint and taking your neighbours to court, it's quicker, free and won't leave the loser with aggressive intentions.

PART 2

You are going to read an extract from a book. For questions **8–15**, choose the answer (**A, B, C** or **D**) which you think fits best according to the text.
Mark your answers **on the separate answer sheet**.

FELICIA'S JOURNEY

Since arriving in the town this morning Felicia has discovered that often she cannot understand what people say because they speak in an accent that is unfamiliar to her. Even when they repeat their statements there is a difficulty, and as often as not she has to give up. She has been told that the best place to find what she is looking for is the industrial area and so she goes there. She makes enquiries in a building that sells office requirements – filing cabinets and revolving chairs as well as paper in bulk and supplies of envelopes and fasteners and transparent tape, everything piled up untidily, not as in a shop. Half of what the girl says in reply escapes her, but she knows it doesn't matter because the girl keeps shaking her head, denying in this way all knowledge of a garden equipment factory.

The industrial area is an endless repetition of unremarkable commercial buildings, each with a forecourt for parking. Its concrete roads are long and straight. Nobody casually walks them for the pleasure of doing so. No dogs meet other dogs. Business is in all directions, buying and selling, discount for cash. It takes Felicia nearly two hours to find Pritchard's Garden Supplies Company.

'An electric machine you're thinking of, is it?' the salesman responds in answer to her query, and she asks if the place is a factory, if the equipment is made here.

'We have our workshops on the premises for after-care. The annual service we recommend, though it's entirely up to you. You'd be going for electric, would you?'

'I'm looking for a friend. He works in the stores of a gardening equipment factory.'

The man's manner changes. He can't help her, he states flatly, disappointment emptying his tone of expression.

'Someone I met said you might be able to tell me where a factory was.'

'Our machines are manufactured in works all over the country. I'm sorry. I believe someone else requires my attention.'

A couple are measuring garden furniture with a dressmaking tape. They want something for their conservatory, Felicia hears them informing the salesman as she goes away.

A man in a car showroom is patient with her but doesn't know of a gardening equipment factory in the vicinity. Then an afterthought strikes him as she's leaving and he mentions the name of a town that he says is twenty-five or six miles off. When it occurs to him that she's puzzled by what he's saying he writes the name down on the edge of a brochure. 'Not very bright' is something her father often says about people. She wonders if the man is thinking that.

No one else can help her. She walks through the industrial area, investigating every road, enquiring at a builders' firm and in Britannia Computers. In OK Carpets Limited a woman draws a map for her, but when she follows the arrows on it she finds herself at a paint supply warehouse that is closed. She returns to Pritchard's Garden Supplies in the hope that the salesman isn't busy now. More annoyed than before, he ignores her.

She walks wearily back to the town, on the grass verge beside a wide main road. An endless chain of lorries and cars passes close, the noise of their engines a roar that every few moments rises to a crescendo, their headlights on because it has become foggy. The grass she walks on is grey, in places black, decorated by the litter that is scattered all around her – crushed cigarette packets, plastic bags, cans and bottles, crumpled sheets from newspapers, and cartons. In the middle of the morning she had a cup of tea and a piece of fruit cake; she hasn't had anything since and she doesn't feel hungry, but she knows that as soon as she arrives back in the town she will have to find somewhere to stay. Her arms ache from the weight of the two carrier-bags; her feet are sore, blisters in two different places, one of her heels skinned. She knew it wouldn't be easy; even before she set out she knew it wouldn't be; she didn't expect anything else. What has happened is her own fault, due to her own foolishness in not making certain she had an address. She can't blame anyone else.

8 When Felicia goes to the building selling office requirements,

    A   she does not need to understand everything the girl says to her.
    B   the girl cannot remember the way to the garden equipment factory.
    C   she is surprised by the disorganized state of the place.
    D   the girl gets annoyed that Felicia cannot understand her.

9 What do we learn about Felicia in the first paragraph?

    A   She keeps trying to understand what she is told.
    B   She is in a place that she does not know.
    C   She has difficulty in expressing herself.
    D   She feels that people treat her badly.

10 What does the writer say about the industrial area?

    A   There are not usually many people there.
    B   It is typical of all industrial areas.
    C   It is not an attractive place to look at.
    D   There is a long distance between the buildings there.

11 What happens when Felicia first goes to Pritchard's?

    A   The salesman supposes that she has come to buy something.
    B   She misunderstands something that the salesman says to her.
    C   The salesman pretends that he has something else to do.
    D   She fails to make clear to the salesman what she wants.

12 What happens when she goes into other buildings in the industrial area?

    A   She starts to get annoyed.
    B   She does not expect useful information.
    C   She does not believe what she is told.
    D   She makes no progress.

13 When she is walking along the main road, Felicia realizes that

    A   she should have something to eat.
    B   the place is dirtier than she expected.
    C   the traffic is heavier than she is used to.
    D   she still has further difficulties to face.

14 What happens to Felicia in the extract?

    A   Everyone she meets is unfriendly towards her.
    B   She keeps being sent to the wrong places.
    C   Nobody she meets can give her the information she needs.
    D   She keeps being given the wrong information.

15 What do we learn about Felicia in the extract as a whole?

    A   She is not very good at following directions she is given.
    B   She has failed to do something she should have done.
    C   She is a person who frequently makes silly mistakes.
    D   She has difficulty in dealing with people in general.

PART 3

You are going to read a magazine article about a writer of musicals. Eight paragraphs have been removed from the article. Choose from the paragraphs **A–I** the one which fits each gap (**16–22**). There is one extra paragraph which you do not need to use. There is an example at the beginning (**0**). Mark your answers **on the separate answer sheet**.

A better class of musical

It was, admits Anne Dalton cheerfully, a dangerous thing – foolish, even – to do on the point of becoming 40: give up her job as Head of English at a secondary school to try her luck in the theatre, not as a performer but in the even riskier business of writing musicals.

| **0** | *I* |

When *Her Benny* was first staged in Liverpool last July in a semi-professional production, it was financed and directed by Anne herself – and every performance saw 'house full' signs outside the theatre.

| **16** | |

When the theatre manager saw how successful it was, he told his bosses at Apollo Leisure, which controls 19 theatres around the country. As a result, *Her Benny* is being presented in a fully-professional production at the Empire for two weeks from next Tuesday.

| **17** | |

If so, the show's lead roles will continue to be played by operatic tenor Alberto Remedios (Liverpool-born, despite his name) and Sandra Dugdale, who has sung with the English National Opera and in the London production of *The Phantom of the Opera*.

| **18** | |

'The fact that it has everything a good classic story should have', says Anne, 'a struggle for existence, tears and laughter, cruelty and compassion, sympathetic characters, the differing attitudes of the upper and lower classes, morality and a happy ending.'

| **19** | |

She did that while she was still teaching. Then she and Mike went on holiday. 'For various reasons it was a disaster as a holiday,' says Anne. They spent most of their time in the hotel room and Anne filled her hours writing the script.

| **20** | |

'I could do better than that myself,' she declared. And so an interest which soon became an obsession began. But trying to teach by day and compose in her spare time began to affect her health. 'I had to give up one or the other, and really there was no contest. Teaching had to go.'

| **21** | |

At that time, it was also chosen as one of five joint winners, out of a worldwide entry of nearly five hundred, of the International Quest for New Musicals award.

| **22** | |

She claims never to have worked so hard in her life as she has these past few weeks, getting everything ready. 'I sleep well enough at night, because the tension and excitement exhaust me completely. I can't think of anything else. But I wouldn't have missed any of it – not a single second!'

A That was not her first attempt at writing a musical. Her interest had been created when Mike came home one day with the text and music of a show which had been suggested for the children of his school. He thought it pretty awful and so did Anne.

B During its one-week run, it got a wildly applauding, whistling, stamping audience of 14,000. Had the show failed, Anne and her headmaster husband, Mike, could have faced debts of £70,000.

C From her first reading of it, Anne imagined it as a musical. 'I could see immediately where the songs should go, so I wrote them first. All nineteen of them.'

D Anne already has another musical waiting to be produced, based on *The Scarlet Letter* by Nathaniel Hawthorne. 'It's finished and all wrapped up,' she says, 'but it's on the shelf at the moment until we see how *Her Benny* gets on.' She will know soon.

E Invitations for this have gone out to managers, critics and other important people in the theatre world. The hope is that a national tour will follow.

F And so it did – and she hasn't looked back since. The show had its premiere as a concert version in a hotel ballroom. This was followed by amateur performances, and songs from the show were then performed at such non-theatrical venues as the Maritime Museum and Anfield football ground in front of a crowd of nearly 40,000 before a match.

G Based on a sad 19th Century story written by the Reverend Silas K Hocking, it is about two unfortunate children – Benny Bates and his sister, Nelly – who have only their courage and their love for each other to keep them going. What attracted her to it?

H Anne went from teaching English to creativity when she decided to start writing musicals full-time. Since then, her tuneful adaptation of a little-known book has received enthusiastic reviews. But making the decision to give up teaching was not easy.

I That was two years ago. Today, as she walks around Liverpool, she can look up at posters proclaiming 'Anne Dalton's *Her Benny* back by popular demand!'

PART 4

You are going to read a text about consumer rights. For questions **23–33**, choose from the consumer rights (**A–E**). When more than one answer is required, these may be given in any order. There is an example at the beginning (**0**).

For questions **34** and **35**, choose the answer (**A, B, C** or **D**) which you think fits best according to the text.

Mark your answers **on the separate answer sheet**.

In which circumstances are A–E the case, according to the text?

0	*A*	You buy something that you know is faulty and it breaks.
23		Something you have paid for is not delivered on time.
24 25		You decide that you prefer a different model from something you have bought.
26		Something you buy is not the same item as it is said to be.
27 28		You are given something faulty for your birthday.
29		You return something faulty but you have no proof that you bought it.
30		A shop will not let you pay for goods later.
31		You fail to cancel a dinner reservation in advance.
32		You buy something at a reduced price and discover a fault that had not been pointed out.
33		You return something faulty that you bought for someone else.

A The money you paid must be returned to you.

B You may be offered something else.

C You are responsible legally.

D You can demand a detailed explanation.

E You are not entitled to money back.

34 What is the purpose of the text?
- **A** to warn the reader about certain illegal practices
- **B** to explain changes in the law concerning consumers
- **C** to correct possible misunderstandings about the law
- **D** to advise people to be careful when shopping

35 Who is most likely to have produced this text?
- **A** a group of businesses
- **B** a financial organization
- **C** a public advice organization
- **D** a dissatisfied consumer

DO YOU KNOW YOUR CONSUMER RIGHTS?

Try this TRUE or FALSE quiz to see how well you know your rights.

1 You buy a new CD for your daughter's birthday present. When she opens it, the disc is by a different group. The shop has run out of the one you want and says you can have a credit note permitting you to buy goods in the shop to the same value but not a refund. They are right.

TRUE OR FALSE?

2 You buy a casserole dish in a sale. It is labelled 'seconds' and is half the original price. The first time you put it in the oven it falls to pieces. You cannot ask for your money back because you knew it was imperfect when you bought it.

TRUE OR FALSE?

3 You buy a new kettle. When you get it home, you wish you'd bought a cordless one instead. You try to change it but the shop refuses. The shop is within its rights.

TRUE OR FALSE?

4 You can't get a refund on faulty goods if you haven't got the receipt.

TRUE OR FALSE?

5 You order and pay for a new swimming costume which you tell the mail order firm you want for your holiday in five weeks' time. It hasn't arrived by then. You can cancel your order and get your money back.

TRUE OR FALSE?

6 You book a table for four at a restaurant but decide you'd rather stay at home. You don't bother to tell the restaurant, which then takes you to court for the profit on four meals. It is entitled to do this.

TRUE OR FALSE?

7 You buy a present for your aunt, who discovers it is faulty. She is entitled to compensation if she takes it back to the shop where you bought it.

TRUE OR FALSE?

8 You need a new bed and want to pay on credit. The shop refuses you a loan and will not tell you why. It is within its rights.

TRUE OR FALSE?

ANSWERS

1 FALSE. If you take the CD back straight away you can get a refund. Goods must be as described.

2 FALSE. Something marked as seconds will not be perfect but it should still be of saleable quality, as described and fit for its purpose. You cannot be expected to know about hidden faults.

3 TRUE. You are not entitled to a refund just because you change your mind. Some shops, however, will give you a refund or replacement in the interests of good public relations.

4 FALSE. Your rights aren't affected if you don't have a receipt – but it's useful to have one to avoid disputes. You could also use a cheque book stub or a credit card slip, for instance, to prove payment.

5 TRUE. Goods must be delivered within a reasonable time or by an agreed date. Otherwise you have the right to cancel.

6 TRUE. When you book a table, you make a contract with the restaurant. If you don't turn up, you have broken a contract and could be prosecuted for any loss of profit suffered by the restaurant.

7 FALSE. Only the person who bought the item is entitled to compensation. The shop might change the item as a favour.

8 TRUE. But if you ask, the shop must tell you the name and address of any credit reference agency which was asked for information about you. You can write to the agency and ask to see a copy of their file on you.

Paper 2 Writing (1 hour 30 minutes)

PART 1

You **must** answer this question.

1   You and a friend recently spent a few days in London, as part of a touring holiday. While you were there you both wanted to see a good show at the theatre. However, you were not happy with the arrangements the travel company made for you.

Read the advertisement below carefully, and look at the tickets and your comments. Then write a letter to the travel company, explaining why you were not happy with the service they gave.

Only cinema available.

Ask for money back?

As part of our holiday service, we also arrange tickets for one of the top London shows – musicals, ballet, opera – whatever is to your taste!

We book the tickets – all **you** have to do is sit back and enjoy the show!

Choosing a holiday with **CITY TRAVEL** means having a good time out on the town!

PRIORY CINEMA
PRIORY CINEMA 3
Row A 2

Terrible seats!

Couldn't see!

Write a **letter** of **120–180** words in an appropriate style. Do not write any addresses.

PART 2

Write an answer to **one** of the questions **2–5** in this part. Write your answer in **120–180** words in an appropriate style, putting the question number in the box.

---

2   Some English friends of yours are planning a short walking holiday in a part of the country near where you live. They will be sleeping in cheap hotels and each carrying just one small bag of clothes and other equipment.

Write a **letter** to your friends, giving them some useful information about the countryside and the weather they will probably have, and some advice on what to pack.

3   A Canadian university is doing some work on young people's attitudes towards reading. They are asking you to write down your reactions to this statement:

Reading books is a waste of time. There are lots of better ways of studying and using your free time these days.

Write a **composition**, giving your personal opinions and explaining why you agree or disagree with the statement.

4   Two people from another country are visiting the company where you work for a few days. As they are a similar age to you, your boss has asked you to write a report, giving your ideas on what evening activities could be organized for them.

Write your **report**, making at least two suggestions.

5   **Background reading texts**

Answer **one** of the following two questions based on your reading of **one** of the set books. Write the title of the book next to the question number box.

5(a)   Describe the event or events in the book which you have read which you find especially exciting or interesting.

5(b)   If you could add one picture to the book which you have read, which scene from the story would it show? Describe the picture in detail.

Paper 3 Use of English (1 hour 15 minutes)

PART 1

For questions **1–15**, read the text below and decide which word or phrase **A, B, C** or **D** best fits each space. There is an example at the beginning (**0**). Mark your answers **on the separate answer sheet**.

Example:

0   **A**   sailed   **B**   held   **C**   crossed   **D**   made

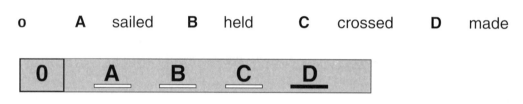

THE QE2

Samuel Cunard's first ship, the *Britannia*, **(0)** .... its first voyage from Liverpool in England to the US in 1850. In those days there was little choice about **(1)** .... of travel. Anyone who **(2)** .... to go to the US from Britain had to sail across the Atlantic. **(3)** .... that, there was no way of getting there. The *Britannia* was **(4)** .... a mail ship, but it also **(5)** .... passengers. On that first **(6)** .... , as records show, there was a **(7)** .... of 63 of them, including Samuel Cunard and his daughter and, **(8)** .... for that time, the ship had private bathrooms.

But Samuel Cunard would find it hard to **(9)** .... much similarity between his beloved *Britannia* and the Cunard company's most famous liner today, the QE2, named after Queen Elizabeth II of England. The *Britannia* is **(10)** .... to have had two members of staff **(11)** .... every passenger. The passengers probably didn't sleep in cabins as comfortable and with as much **(12)** .... as rooms in a good **(13)** .... of hotel, as they do on the QE2 today.

The QE2 **(14)** .... on her first voyage across the Atlantic from Southampton on the south coast of England on May 2 1969. Five days later, she arrived in New York to an enthusiastic **(15)** .... . Since that day she has carried over one and a half million passengers around the world.

1	**A** procedures	**B** processes	**C** courses	**D** means
2	**A** thought	**B** wished	**C** dreamed	**D** fancied
3	**A** Apart from	**B** Else	**C** Instead of	**D** Otherwise
4	**A** at most	**B** above all	**C** overall	**D** vastly
5	**A** fetched	**B** brought	**C** took	**D** sent
6	**A** incident	**B** occasion	**C** event	**D** circumstance
7	**A** total	**B** sum	**C** number	**D** quantity
8	**A** distinctly	**B** differently	**C** extremely	**D** remarkably
9	**A** see	**B** know	**C** tell	**D** catch
10	**A** doubtful	**B** improbable	**C** uncertain	**D** unlikely
11	**A** to	**B** with	**C** by	**D** of
12	**A** breadth	**B** space	**C** extent	**D** expansion
13	**A** level	**B** status	**C** class	**D** rank
14	**A** set off	**B** went away	**C** got out	**D** came along
15	**A** meeting	**B** applause	**C** welcome	**D** acceptance

PART 2

For questions **16–30**, read the text below and think of the word which best fits each space. Use only **one** word in each space. There is an example at the beginning (**0**).
Write your word **on the separate answer sheet**.

Example: | **0** | *with* |

Intuition

Sometimes you just know things about people the first time you see them – for example that you want to be friends (**0**) .... them or that you don't trust them. But perhaps this kind of intuition isn't as hard to explain (**16**) .... it may seem. For instance, everybody gives out body language signals (**17**) .... the time. The (**18**) .... you hold your body, head and arms tells people about your mood. If you hold your arms tightly at your sides (**19**) .... fold them across your chest, people will generally feel that you (**20**) .... being defensive. Holding your head on one side shows interest in the (**21**) .... person, while (**22**) .... relaxed, 'open' posture indicates that you are self-confident. All this affects (**23**) .... we feel about someone.

Also, a stranger may (**24**) .... you of a previous meeting with someone. This may be because of (**25**) .... as simple as the fact that he or she is physically similar (**26**) .... someone who treated you well – or badly. But your reaction doesn't (**27**) .... to be the result of the memory of a person you previously met – your feelings about the stranger could (**28**) .... influenced by a smell in the air that brings to mind a place (**29**) .... you were happy as a child. Since even a single word can bring back a memory (**30**) .... as that, you may never realise it is happening.

PART 3

For questions **31–40**, complete the second sentence so that it has a similar meaning to the first sentence. Use the word given and other words to complete the sentence. **You must not use more than five words. Do not change the word given.** There is an example at the beginning (**0**).
Write **only** the missing words **on the separate answer sheet**.

Example:

0 'Do you know how to get to the town centre?' she asked me.

way

She asked me .... to the town centre.

The gap can be filled with the words

| **0** | *whether I knew the way* | OR | **0** | *if I knew the way* |

---

31 While I was driving, I realized that the car wasn't working properly.

wrong

While I was driving, I realized that .... the car.

32 I couldn't go to work because of the transport strike.

prevented

I .... to work by the transport strike.

33 I was the only person who wanted to watch the programme.

else

There was .... me who wanted to watch the programme.

34 He watched videos all day.

entire

He spent .... videos.

35 It will be necessary to pay the full amount when you book.

have

The full amount .... when you book.

85

36   I didn't see her again for five years.

before

Five years had .... her again.

37   I don't think she likes doing other people's work for them.

objects

I think .... other people's work for them.

38   Jeremy frequently invents ridiculous stories like that!

make

It is typical .... a ridiculous story like that!

39   The police think that he was one of the robbers.

taking

The police suspect .... the robbery.

40   Because he was so proud, he couldn't admit that he was wrong.

too

He had .... that he was wrong.

PART 4

For questions **41–55**, read the text below and look carefully at each line. Some of the lines are correct, and some have a word which should not be there.
If a line is correct, put a tick (✓) by the number **on the separate answer sheet**.
If a line has a word which should **not** be there, write the word **on the separate answer sheet**. There are two examples at the beginning (**0**) and (**00**).

Examples:

0	*are*
00	✓

Pop Music

0	Most people are agree that pop music started in the US in the 1950s and
00	that it developed from black American music. When it started, it was
41	especially for young people. In many countries they liked listening to it and
42	dancing to it because it was exciting and it was highly a way of rebelling
43	against their parents' generation. Many of parents strongly disapproved
44	of it. They disliked the way many pop stars looked like and acted. They
45	thought as the music was rubbish and the groups couldn't sing or play
46	their instruments properly neither. They said that pop music wouldn't last
47	for long time. Today, attitudes are different. Many of today's parents are
48	people who loved pop music when they were young, and still do love. As a
49	result of this, pop music is no longer only for the young. In addition, some
50	of the stars whose careers began a long time ago and who they are now
51	middle-aged are just as popular today as they were at then. Their original
52	fans still like them, perhaps because they remind them of when they
53	were young. At the same time, either new generations of young people buy
54	their records and go to their concerts. So that pop music was not just a
55	brief fashion. All these years later, it is more popular than for ever.

PART 5

For questions **56–65**, read the text below. Use the word given in capitals at the end of each line to form a word that fits in the space in the same line. There is an example at the beginning (**0**).
Write your word **on the separate answer sheet**.

Example: | **0** | *responsibility* |

Women Doctors

Throughout history, women have had (**0**) .... for healing the sick.	**RESPONSIBLE**
However, it is only in (**56**) .... recent times that they have been	**COMPARE**
allowed to train as doctors at (**57**) .... schools in Britain. Yet in that	**MEDICINE**
short time, they have made an enormous (**58**) .... to modern medicine.	**CONTRIBUTE**
The first female doctors were priestesses who gave (**59**) .... about	**ADVISE**
diseases and (**60**) .... and prepared medicines. In ancient Rome, women	**INJURE**
healers were considered (**61**) .... and respected.	**SKILL**
In Britain, for centuries male doctors were (**62**) .... of women who	**SUSPECT**
practised medicine (**63**) .... and in 1512 a law was passed making it	**PROFESSION**
(**64**) .... for them to do so. Women couldn't study medicine at	**LEGAL**
universities until the 19th Century and they only began to gain (**65**)	**EQUAL**
with male doctors in the 20th century.	

Paper 4 Listening (approximately 40 minutes)

PART 1

You will hear people talking in eight different situations.
For questions **1–8**, choose the best answer **A, B** or **C**.

1 You hear a critic on the radio talking about a book. What is his main criticism of the book?

   A The style is poor.

   B The plot is too complicated.

   C The characters are not believable.

2 You hear someone talking about a time when she was a student abroad. What did she particularly like?

   A the school she studied at

   B the town she stayed in

   C the family she stayed with

3 You hear a radio interviewer introducing a guest. Who is the guest?

   A a scientist

   B a businessman

   C an inventor

4 You hear a caller on a radio phone-in programme. What feeling does the caller express?

   A sympathy

   B self-pity

   C envy

5 You hear part of a radio interview. Who is being interviewed?

   A a customer at a shop

   B the manager of a shop

   C someone who lives near a shop

6 You hear someone talking on a public telephone. What does she want the other person to do?

   A explain something he said

   B apologize to someone

   C give an honest opinion

7 You hear someone talking at the Information Desk in an airport. What is his situation?

   A He has missed his flight.

   B He has come to meet someone.

   C He thinks there is a message for him.

8 You hear the presenter talking at the beginning of a radio programme. What is the programme going to be about?

   A how to eat healthily

   B new food products

   C eating habits

PART 2

You will hear a talk given to a class by a young woman, in which she talks about her career so far as an actress and director.
For questions **9–18**, fill in the missing information.

THE ACTRESS-DIRECTOR

university course: | **9** |

most of her acting course was: | **10** |

first job: did | **11** | work

then wrote many letters to: | **12** |

next job: did not improve her

| **13** |

first play as director: received | **14** |

next play as director: won award for | **15** |

then tried to get a job in: | **16** |

would now like to be employed by: | **17** |

had not expected: | **18** | for so long

PART 3

You will hear five different people talking about a concert on a radio phone-in programme.
For questions **19–23**, choose from the list **A–F** what each speaker is doing.
Use the letters only once. There is one extra letter which you do not need to use.

A asking for opinions

B disagreeing with an opinion

C correcting some details

D asking for advice

E making a complaint

F making a recommendation

Speaker 1	19
Speaker 2	20
Speaker 3	21
Speaker 4	22
Speaker 5	23

PART 4

You will hear an interview with two young people who spent some time travelling abroad.

For questions **24–30**, write **D** next to what Dan says, **A** next to what Anna says and **N** next to what neither of them says.

24   I particularly enjoyed the first part of my trip.

25   I sometimes lost my temper.

26   I was disappointed by some of the places I went to.

27   I stayed in some unpleasant places.   27

28   I learnt from the experiences of others.   28

29   I lost interest in my trip.

30   Travelling alone is the best way to travel.

Paper 5 Speaking (15 minutes for 2 candidates)

(about 4 minutes)

Practise answering these questions.

What do you like doing in your spare time?
Do you have any special hobbies?
Do you play any sports?
Would you like to do any of these things as a career?
What would be the ideal job for you?

(about 4 minutes)

Both candidates should look at pictures 4A and 4B on page 126.

The pictures show two different types of holiday.

Candidate A

Compare and contrast these pictures, saying how you feel about holidays like these. You have about a minute to do this.

Candidate B

Talk about which of these holidays you would prefer to have. You have about 20 seconds to do this.

Both candidates should now look at pictures 4C and 4D on page 126.

The pictures show different places you could go to for a special evening out.

Candidate B

Compare and contrast these pictures, saying which kind of evening out you prefer and why. You have about a minute to do this.

Candidate A

Talk about which kind of evening out you would prefer. You have about 20 seconds to do this.

(about 3 minutes)

Both candidates should look at the set of pictures 4E on page 125.

The pictures show different presents. A mother and father want to choose something nice to give to their teenage daughter on a special occasion. They want to choose something she will be able to keep for many years.

Talk to each other about this and decide which present you think would be best and why. Which do you think would be the worst choice for the parents to make? Why?

(about 4 minutes)

Now think about these questions. Tell each other what your opinions are.

• Which are the occasions in your country when people give presents to family and friends?

• Has anyone ever given you a really special present? What was it?

• Do you prefer a present to be a surprise, or do you like to choose what you are given?

• What things do you like to give to your friends as presents?

• What are the most useful things for parents to give their children?

Test 5

PART 1

You are going to read a magazine article about making decisions. Choose the most suitable heading from the list **A–H** for each part (**1–6**) of the article. There is one extra heading which you do not need to use. There is an example at the beginning (**0**).

Mark your answers **on the separate answer sheet**.

A	Any decision is better than none
B	It's not up to anyone else
C	Admit it when you've made the wrong choice
D	Fear of what may result
E	False beliefs
F	Follow your own judgements
G	The best approach
H	Everyone has to make decisions

DECISIONS, DECISIONS

0	*H*

We have to make choices every day of our lives – whether it's what to have for lunch or choosing between the red or the black jacket. Do you make up your mind quickly or are you one of life's ditherers? The difference between having a tuna or chicken sandwich isn't going to change the world, but sometimes you have to make an important decision that will have a long-term impact on your life.

1	

Deciding whether to go to college or leave your job and go travelling is not easy when you've got no experience to base your decision on. After all, how do you know what backpacking around Borneo will be like if you've never done it? What's more, you've probably got everyone telling you what they think you should do. Their advice may sound sensible, but if your heart says no, it's not the right choice for you. Learning to make your own mind up is about becoming an adult. When we're young, our parents do a lot of our decision-making for us, but as we grow up we take responsibility for ourselves. However, grabbing the power to make decisions for ourselves means taking responsibility for the consequences – even when things go wrong.

2	

People become indecisive because they don't want to do the wrong thing. You change your mind constantly, write endless lists of pros and cons, seek advice from everyone and end up horribly confused. The truth is that you're terrified of making a mistake – and the bigger the decision, the bigger the potential mistake. For example, if you buy a horrible pair of boots, you know that all you've done is waste a week's spending money. But if

you buy a flat with someone and living together turns out to be a nightmare, you could end up involved in a financial and emotional mess.

3	

But the fact is that there's an element of chance in every decision, so often our gut feelings are the only thing we've got to guide us. Whatever you decide at the time is right; it's only in the light of what happens next that it can seem wrong. If you decide to spend your hard-earned money on a battered old car and three months later it falls to bits, you'll think you made a terrible decision. But if it goes along for years, you'll congratulate yourself. So stop trying to predict the future and trust your instincts.

4	

Decisive people command respect because they know what they think. You may think it's amusing to have a reputation for being indecisive, but eventually you'll drive others mad. Indecisive people lack personal power because they appear unreliable, out of control and even selfish. If you're always causing people trouble because you change your mind at the last minute, you'll seem unreliable. Decisive people are successful because they make a decision and move on – and if it doesn't go the way they planned, they make the best of it.

5	

● **Do all the research you need**

If you want to move out of home, work out exactly how much it will cost before taking such a big step.

● **What's your gut feeling?**

Maybe you're desperate to study drama but your parents are keen on Business

Studies. Remember, you know yourself best.

● **Set yourself a time limit**

If you're choosing which film to see, give yourself five minutes; if you're deciding whether to go travelling, set a deadline and stick to it.

● **Be firm**

Once you've made your choice, tell people about it and stick to it. Decisive people command respect because they say they're going to do something and they do it.

● **Don't look back**

Put all your energy into planning your choice. That way you'll forget there was ever another option. Don't waste time picturing what might have been if you'd taken a different path.

6	

● **'Once you've made a decision, it can never be altered.'**

Many of us live with the notion that any big decision we make is set in concrete – that we only get one opportunity and if we get it wrong, we'll be a failure. Of course, this isn't true. If you go in one direction and hate it, change.

● **'There's no hurry.'**

The sooner you make a decision, the better. Don't wait until three days before the holidays to choose a destination, then be panicked into going somewhere you don't want.

● **'This is the biggest decision of your life.'**

If you believe this, you will be paralysed with indecision. Most choices seem crucial when you're making them, but remember – no one decision is going to affect you forever.

PART 2

You are going to read a magazine article about a flying instructor. For questions **7–13**, choose the answer (**A, B, C** or **D**) which you think fits best according to the text.

Mark your answers **on the separate answer sheet**.

High Flying

Six years ago Susie O'Hara was a high flying Sales and Marketing Director when she treated herself to a trial flying lesson. She took to it instantly. Since then Susie has spent £40,000 on her habit. Eight months ago she gave up her job to become a professional flying instructor at the EFG Flying School. She has had to let her home and is staying with her mother. Her salary last year before stoppages was around £6,000. 'I could earn more doing any other job, like cleaning...,' Susie shrugs. 'It turned my lifestyle upside down. All my friends thought I was mad. But I just wanted to fly the whole time. I figured I had to do it now or I would be too old.'

So how good can flying be to possess someone to give up everything? To get your basic licence you are looking at spending £4,000 plus. Besides the time actually spent flying, there is a lot of homework and you must pass written exams on every aspect of flying from law and meteorology to technical papers on the aeroplanes and the limits of the human body. Susie has so far sat 31 professional exams.

'Part of the appeal is the different view it gives you of life,' she says. 'Sometimes when you're up there and you can see everything so tiny below, you realise everyone has their problems and that so many problems are so small. It's not like that all the time but sometimes that hits you.'

Another aspect may be the glamorous lifestyle. France is only half an hour from the airfield and southern Spain is also a popular destination. To collect enough hours to get her commercial licence, Susie used to stay out in the US after business trips, where flying is very cheap, and has flown from Long Beach to Las Vegas and from Florida across the Bahamas. Flying in the US is so cheap that a lot of people go there to collect their air miles.

It's a beautiful day when I try it. Once you're off the ground you can see for miles – only the horizon is lost in a white haze. You're aware that the ground is way down there, and there's that feeling in your stomach and your ears are popping. A great deal of the appeal is the amazing acrobatics you can do. One minute you weigh several times your normal weight, the next you are seemingly weightless. The earth spins confusingly somewhere over your shoulder as you do sudden 180 degree turns. 'It's a pity this is not really an acrobatic plane,' says Susie, 'because that is what I really love.'

As well as acrobatics Susie pretends the engine has stalled and goes through the process of a crash landing. She also gives me a chance to handle the plane. It's amazing how responsive it is. By the way, before you take off in a lesson, you go through a lot of the theory on the ground, as I had.

When we land I feel a little sick. But I asked for it – the acrobatics are optional. 'You have to know the other person can deal with it before you do acrobatics,' says Susie. More than anything I'm disappointed the whole episode is over so quickly. The entire time the flight had an air of unreality about it. I can understand its appeal. I'm less sure whether the experience is really worth sacrificing as much as Susie has. Roller coaster rides in funfairs offer you the same feelings for a small percentage of the price. But then there's more to it than that.

7   What do we learn about Susie in the first paragraph?

    A   She regrets the financial disadvantages of becoming a flying instructor.

    B   She was upset by criticism of her decision to become a flying instructor.

    C   She felt she could not put off the decision to become a flying instructor.

    D   She had always been planning to become a flying instructor eventually.

8   What does the writer emphasize about becoming a flying instructor in the second paragraph?

    A   that it is more difficult than some people think it is

    B   that few people are able to make the necessary sacrifices

    C   that being able to fly is only one of the many things involved

    D   that few people are capable of achieving what is required

9   One reason why Susie enjoys flying is that

    A   it makes her feel more important.

    B   it helps her solve her problems.

    C   it has increased her self-confidence.

    D   it gives her a realistic view of life.

10   Why did Susie fly in the US?

    A   It was a good way of making progress towards qualifying.

    B   She met a lot of other people like herself there.

    C   She liked the places that she could fly to there.

    D   It gave her practice at flying in a different country.

11   What was the main thing the writer noticed during his flight with Susie?

    A   how much skill Susie had at doing acrobatics

    B   the number of physical sensations he experienced

    C   how much it differed from what he had expected

    D   the variety of skills involved in flying a plane

12   When the writer took over the controls of the plane,

    A   he had to practise an emergency landing.

    B   he found it difficult to get it under control.

    C   he already knew something about flying a plane.

    D   he became so nervous that he felt ill afterwards.

13   What does the writer say at the end of the article about learning to fly?

    A   It is possible to appreciate what makes people want to do it.

    B   His lesson was too short for him to draw any conclusions about it.

    C   Only a certain kind of person is attracted to doing it.

    D   The cost involved makes it unattractive to many people.

PART 3

You are going to read a newspaper article about travel writers. Eight sentences have been removed from the article. Choose from the sentences **A–I** the one which fits each gap (**14–20**). There is one extra sentence which you do not need to use. There is an example at the beginning (**0**).
Mark your answers **on the separate answer sheet**.

Travel notes

Write notes or take photographs? Sketch or draw from memory? Travel writers talk to Mike Gerrard about their methods.

For most of us, the thought of even writing a few postcards home is a nuisance when travelling abroad. But what of the travel writer who has a whole book to write? Writing a daily notebook creates problems of a totally different order.

'The problem in Siberia', says Christina Dodwell of the trip which produced *Beyond Siberia*, 'was that the ink in my pen froze. | **0** | *I* | And up in the mist on Mount Ararat I found that that was the only thing that would write on damp paper.'

The superiority of the humble pencil is something also discovered by Eric Newby. | **14** | He wrote *A Short Walk in the Hindu Kush* 'all in pencil, which was fortunate as my horse went into a river and most of my films were ruined. My book would have been, too, if I'd written it in pen, because all the colour would have run.'

'I did a similar thing when I went down the Ganges. I got a huge Gujurati account book, bound in red cotton, a very stout thing with a piece of rope round it to shut it. First I wrote about minor things, like 'saw a tree', 'saw a cow', because there wasn't much in the upper part of the Ganges. | **15** | '

Where Newby's writing expanded, Dodwell's shrank. 'Over the years my writing has got smaller and smaller, so I can now get two lines per line on lined paper. | **16** | Keeping the notes small means there's less of a bundle to carry – and less of a bundle to lose.'

Bill Bryson has taken this even further, and virtually given up making notes altogether. 'Because *The Lost Continent* was my first travel book', he says, 'I set off taking notes about absolutely everything. However, I found myself sitting in a café one morning writing down 'spent time in a café writing down notes.' | **17** | '

'Instead, I now take lots and lots of pictures – not very good ones, but good enough to remind me of what somewhere like Nebraska looks like. The only notes I take now are occasional funny phrases, if they occur to me. Sometimes something will strike me as interesting or amusing and I write down things like 'Don't forget fat man in red trousers'. | **18** | '

Where Bryson takes photographs, Jan Morris has another way of remembering things. 'I always use small hardback notebooks and a felt-tip pen, because I like to do drawings to remind me what things look like. The notes tend to be little impressions, but do form a lot of what goes into the books.'

What would she do if she lost her notes? 'I'd be incredibly upset. | **19** | However, talking to you now has got me worried.'

Norman Lewis keeps his notes safely packed away with his passport and tickets, while Redmond O'Hanlon says ' | **20** | But then, that's how you feel about everything you've got in the jungle, which is where I mostly travel. You get ridiculously worried about your knife, your boots – everything's a worry in the jungle. I neurotically tape my notes inside the lining of my pack, but you're as likely to lose a pack as your notes.'

A   So then I began doing less of that.

B   Later, there was more of interest and it became full of explanations, conversations and descriptions of rituals.

C   I do get nervous about losing my notebook.

D   It also makes it impossible for other people to read, which can be quite an advantage.

E   It is for my book and of no interest to anyone else.

F   Unfortunately, when I come to write a book I often have no recollection of why I made these notes.

G   This was something that happened by accident.

H   I don't do anything to make sure I don't lose my notes.

I   I got round the problem by using a pencil.

PART 4

You are going to read a magazine article in which various newspaper editors are interviewed.

For questions **21–35**, choose from the editors (**A–E**). Some of the editors may be chosen more than once. There is an example at the beginning (**0**).

Mark your answers **on the separate answer sheet**.

Which of the editors states the following?

I find it surprising that strangers sometimes know who I am.	**0**	*C*
I always like arriving for work.	**21**	
Newspapers should cheer people up.	**22**	
I expect my staff to work hard.	**23**	
My influence can be seen in my newspaper.	**24**	
I have achieved all my aims.	**25**	
An editor should have firm opinions.	**26**	
I sometimes want to do less work.	**27**	
Rules about what I can do annoy me.	**28**	
Editors shouldn't lead glamorous lives.	**29**	
Staff can come to see me most of the time.	**30**	
Newspapers should not have too much serious content.	**31**	
The effect newspapers have should not be overestimated.	**32**	
I have the final responsibility for everything.	**33**	
An editor should always be cheerful.	**34**	
If you stop enjoying the job, you should give it up.	**35**	

A   Alan

B   Barbara

C   Colin

D   David

E   Elizabeth

NEWSPAPER EDITORS TALKING

THE EDITORS

ALAN BROWN is the editor of the *Daily Standard*.
BARBARA LONG is the editor of the *Correspondent*.
COLIN WILSON edits the *Daily Globe*.
DAVID JOHNSON edits the *Sunday Chronicle*.
ELIZABETH LESTER is the editor of the *Sunday Post*.

Essential for the job

Alan   You need to understand your readers absolutely. You've got to reflect all their hopes, dreams, fears and anxieties. You've got to bring a bit of sunshine into their lives – a laugh, a smile, occasionally a tear.

Barbara   You can't lunch in expensive restaurants or spend every evening in clubs. You have to be down to earth and in touch with what people think and feel.

Colin   You basically have to be what your readers are. You have to have the same aspirations and standards. Deep down, I'm the same person as the men and women who buy the *Daily Globe*.

David   Attitude: knowing what you like and what you don't like. Being on the side of the reader and reflecting what they want, as well as guiding them.

Elizabeth   You've got to be sharp, understanding and have a lot of energy. And never be down.

Being the boss

Barbara   I'm very hands-on. I don't sit in my office and think it's great to be an editor. I make staff believe they can achieve.

Colin   I tell a lot of jokes. I've done away with management structures. My door is rarely closed.

David   I go out on the floor and chat to the reporters, sub-editors and feature writers. It's very important, communication.

Elizabeth   You have to motivate staff. It's a tight-knit team, but, as the editor, in the end I'm the one in charge.

Getting Tough

Alan   Some people have described me as the toughest person they've ever met.

My bootprint is stamped on this paper more than any other editor's on any other paper.

Barbara   When I came to the paper it was getting old, so it was a situation where I had to make radical changes. I didn't find it difficult to sack people who had been sitting around doing nothing. I didn't feel guilty if they were taking four-hour lunches and going off home at 6pm.

Colin   Like all people who claim to be democrats, I'm actually a bit of a dictator. I don't really suffer fools gladly, although I may be one myself. Frankly, the paper had been doing terribly for years and we had to change radically.

Power and influence

Alan   It's nonsense to say that we influence opinions. You can't make people do something they don't want to do. What you can do is inform people about what's going on.

Barbara   It's a two-way thing. Newspapers influence people but people influence newspapers too.

Elizabeth   The *Sunday Post* can highlight aspects of society that need putting right, but at the same time, newspapers are there to entertain.

The highs

Alan   I get a tremendous thrill out of this job. I never come in and think, 'Oh no, another day'. Sometimes it's a battle and you're caught in the crossfire – but it's very exciting.

Barbara   The biggest pleasure is standing in a newsagent's on a Sunday morning seeing people buying the paper. The day you lose that excitement is the day you should say, 'I shouldn't be doing this job any more.'

Colin   It's not power, it's the ability to change things. I'm a romantic, and it's a

wonderful feeling to know that if you work hard enough and shout loud enough, you are going to make a difference. I've also taken my family around the world and done lots of exciting, extraordinary things.

David   The best thing is to have created an interesting, stimulating newspaper which will influence other people.

Elizabeth   The high point is the excitement and variety of things to do.

The lows

Alan   I work ridiculously long hours. There are times when I think, 'What on earth am I doing?' I don't get any time off and I'm weary, but then something happens and I think, 'Great, I'm off again.'

Barbara   When I had my son, I only stayed off work for a week. It was easier. If I'd stayed with him for three months I couldn't have come back to work. But you either love it or you hate it.

Colin   It never fails to amaze me when people recognize me. It brings it home that I am editor of the *Daily Globe*, and it is everything I wanted to do. It frightens me a little bit that I have realised that final ambition.

David   I don't ever feel tired. I feel I'm doing a worthwhile job. If I get worn out, I go on holiday.

Elizabeth   What gets me down is when you have a good story and for whatever reason – often legal, these days – you can't publish it in the way you want.

Paper 2 Writing (1 hour 30 minutes)

PART 1

You **must** answer this question.

---

1   You have arranged to go on a language course next month at a college in Dublin. Now a letter from your friend Mo, who lives in Dublin, has arrived, and Mo wants you to change your arrangements. You are going to write to the college to try to do this.

Read carefully the part of the letter from Mo and the note from the college. Then write your letter to the course secretary, asking whether it is possible to change your arrangements and explaining why you want to do this.

Delighted to hear that you will be arriving in Dublin on July 10. Only one problem! I'm off on holiday for two weeks on July 12! Can't you start your course a day late? It's our only chance to have a day together. Also, why don't you stay in my flat while I'm away? It will be nicer and cheaper than getting accommodation through the college.

Love,

Mo

As requested, we have booked a place for you on the full-time course 'Holiday English', beginning on Monday, July 11, and ending on Friday, July 22. Accommodation with a local family has been arranged from Sunday, July 10 (details on separate sheet).

Please arrive at the college at 9.30 a.m. on the morning of July 11.

Yours sincerely

Cynthia Canter
Cynthia Canter (Course Secretary)

Write a **letter** of **120–180** words in an appropriate style. Do not write any addresses.

PART 2

Write an answer to **one** of the questions **2–5** in this part. Write your answer in **120–180** words in an appropriate style, putting the question number in the box.

---

2   You have been asked to write an article for a guide book for English-speaking tourists. It is called *The Brief Guide* and all the articles in it give advice on what people should try to do and see if they have only one day to spend in a place.

Write your **article**, giving advice to tourists about a town or city you know well.

3   It is World Environment Week. Because of this, your English teacher has asked all the students in your class to write about their opinions on this statement:

The biggest dangers to our health and environment come from cars.

Write your **composition**, saying whether you agree or disagree with the statement and giving examples.

4   An international organization is raising money to help poor children, by producing a book called *My First Day At School*. In the book, people from many different countries describe their memories of their first day at school. You are one of the people chosen to write about your own memories of that day.

Write your **account** for the book.

5   **Background reading texts**

Answer **one** of the following two questions based on your reading of **one** of the set books. Write the title of the book next to the question number box.

5(a)   If you could speak to the author of the book which you have read, what would you like to say? Which questions would you ask? Write a **letter** to the author.

5(b)   Which period in history is the book which you have read set in? How does this affect the characters and events of the story?

Paper 3 Use of English (1 hour 15 minutes)

PART 1

For questions **1–15**, read the text below and decide which word or phrase **A, B, C** or **D** best fits each space. There is an example at the beginning (**0**). Mark your answers **on the separate answer sheet**.

Example:

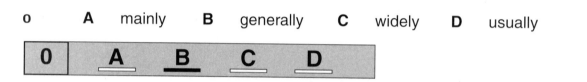

0   **A**   mainly   **B**   generally   **C**   widely   **D**   usually

| 0 | A | B | C | D |

Intelligence Tests

School exams are, **(0)** .... speaking, the first kind of tests we take. They find out how much knowledge we have **(1)** .... . But do they really show how *intelligent* we are? After all, isn't it a **(2)** .... that some people who are very successful academically don't have any **(3)** .... sense?

Intelligence is the speed **(4)** .... which we can understand and **(5)** .... to new situations and it is usually tested by logic puzzles. Although scientists are now preparing **(6)** .... computer technology that will be able to 'read' our brains, **(7)** .... tests are still the most popular ways of measuring intelligence.

A person's IQ is their intelligence **(8)** .... it is measured by a special test. The most common IQ tests are **(9)** .... by Mensa, an organization that was founded in England in 1946. By 1976 it **(10)** .... 1,300 members in Britain. Today there are 44,000 in Britain and 100,000 worldwide, **(11)** .... in the US.

People taking the tests are judged in **(12)** .... to an average score of 100, and those who score over 148 are entitled to join Mensa. This **(13)** .... at 2% of the population. Anyone from the age of six can take the tests. All the questions are straightforward and most people can answer them if **(14)** .... enough time. But that's the problem – the whole **(15)** .... of the tests is that they're against the clock.

1	**A** fetched	**B** gained	**C** attached	**D** caught
2	**A** case	**B** fact	**C** circumstance	**D** truth
3	**A** natural	**B** bright	**C** sharp	**D** common
4	**A** on	**B** to	**C** in	**D** at
5	**A** accord	**B** react	**C** answer	**D** alter
6	**A** advanced	**B** forward	**C** ahead	**D** upper
7	**A** at this age	**B** for the present	**C** at the time	**D** now and then
8	**A** how	**B** that	**C** as	**D** so
9	**A** appointed	**B** commanded	**C** run	**D** steered
10	**A** held	**B** had	**C** kept	**D** belonged
11	**A** largely	**B** enormously	**C** highly	**D** considerably
12	**A** concern	**B** relation	**C** regard	**D** association
13	**A** adds up	**B** turns to	**C** comes up	**D** works out
14	**A** allowed	**B** spared	**C** let	**D** provided
15	**A** reason	**B** point	**C** matter	**D** question

PART 2

For questions **16–30**, read the text below and think of the word which best fits each space. Use only **one** word in each space. There is an example at the beginning (**0**).

Write your word on the **separate answer sheet**.

Example: | **0** | *from* |

Recycling steel cans

Cans made of steel are very easy to remove (**0**) ... domestic rubbish because steel is the only common metal that is attracted to magnets. Many waste removal authorities have (**16**) .... advantage of this fact and have installed large magnets, which, (**17**) .... put it simply, pull all steel containers out of the general household rubbish. The system is known (**18**) .... 'magnetic extraction' and it has two great advantages.

Firstly, unlike most recycling schemes, the recycling (**19**) .... steel cans through 'magnetic extraction' requires almost (**20**) .... effort from the public. As long as you throw your used steel can into the rubbish bin, it will be collected (**21**) .... then the waste removal authority will (**22**) .... the rest. Other packaging cannot be recycled (**23**) .... the public collect the material and take (**24**) .... , usually by car, to a central collection point. This often uses up more energy in petrol than (**25**) .... eventually saved by recycling the material.

Secondly, local authorities actually save public money (**26**) .... recovering used steel cans. Magnetic extraction equipment is simple and cheap, and the steel that has (**27**) .... saved is sold to companies who re-use it (**28**) .... making new steel products. (**29**) .... the value of the metal is greater than the cost of magnetic extraction, the process has financial benefits.

So, magnetic recycling of steel cans from waste saves you time, effort and money, as (**30**) .... as saving energy for us all.

PART 3

For questions **31–40**, complete the second sentence so that it has a similar meaning to the first sentence. Use the word given and other words to complete each sentence. **You must not use more than five words. Do not change the word given**. There is an example at the beginning (**0**).
Write **only** the missing words **on the separate answer sheet**.

Example:

0 'Do you know how to get to the town centre?' she asked me.

way

She asked me .... to the town centre.

The gap can be filled by the words

| **0** | *whether I knew the way* | OR | **0** | *if I knew the way* |

---

31 I strongly advise you to tell her you're sorry.

apologize

I think you'd .... her.

32 It is likely that my friends haven't received my letter yet.

unlikely

My friends .... my letter yet.

33 He seemed to be worried about something.

impression

I .... was worrying him.

34 I've never seen anyone play so skilfully before.

much

I've never seen anyone play .... before.

35 What caused him to change his mind?

reason

What was .... of mind?

36 When should we collect the books we ordered last week?

supposed

When .... up the books we ordered last week?

37 'It's important that you don't tell anyone else what I've told you,' she said to him.

repeat

She urged .... anyone else what she had told him.

38 I was surprised to discover that the hotel was a long way from the city centre.

turned

To .... that the hotel was a long way from the city centre.

39 She would like a job that will allow her to travel abroad a lot.

give

She would like a job that will .... travel abroad a lot.

40 Very few tickets are left, so book now!

hardly

Book now, because .... left!

PART 4

For questions **41–55**, read the text below and look carefully at each line. Some of the lines are correct, and some have a word which should not be there.
If a line is correct put a tick (✓) by the number **on the separate answer sheet**.
If a line has a word which should **not** be there, write the word **on the separate answer sheet**. There are two examples at the beginning (**0**) and (**00**).

Examples:

0	✓
00	*together*

Exchange visits

0	I am writing to you to see whether your school would be interested in taking
00	part in exchange visits with my school together. I am president of our
41	school's Cultural Society and one of our aims is to start relationships with
42	schools in other countries. We have done a research into various cities
43	around the world and it seems as that your city is quite similar to ours.
44	Like for your city, ours is an industrial city and it has a long history.
45	Let me tell you something about it, in case of you haven't heard the
46	name before. It is in the north of England and its industry is by making
47	cars. I expect it that you might have seen some of the cars which are made
48	here in your country. However, there is more to our city than that one – we
49	also have a very good theatre, a number of cinemas and a wide range of
50	sports facilities. We understand that your city is also a nice place to visit. Do
51	you think possible that we could set up an arrangement for exchange visits?
52	There are many families here who would be happy to receive in students
53	from your school for a visit and many of us are keen to visit your city. Do
54	you think there are families at your end who would like to do that the same?
55	Please let me know whether do you think this is a good idea. If so, we can
	start to make arrangements soon.

PART 5

For questions **56–65**, read the text below. Use the word given in capitals at the end of each line to form a word that fits in the space in the same line. There is an example at the beginning (**0**).
Write your word **on the separate answer sheet**.

Example: | **0** | *beauty* |

The Cotswolds

The Cotswolds is an area of great (**0**) .... in England. It has a   **BEAUTIFUL**

number of (**56**) .... villages and small towns with lovely old   **DELIGHT**

buildings that have remained (**57**) .... since the area was a major   **CHANGE**

(**58**) .... centre several centuries ago. The countryside in the area   **COMMERCE**

is (**59**) .... and most of the buildings there are made from an   **CHARM**

(**60**) .... type of light stone that is particular to the Cotswolds.   **ATTRACT**

In the summer, the Cotswolds can get rather (**61**) .... but it is   **CROWD**

always possible to find pretty places that do not have the (**62**) ....   **FAMOUS**

of the more well-known villages and towns. There is no (**63**) .... of   **SHORT**

pleasant hotels and (**64**) .... inns for visitors to stay in and the   **TRADITION**

Cotswolds area is an excellent place for an (**65**) .... weekend   **ENJOY**

or longer trip.

Paper 4 Listening (approximately 40 minutes)

PART 1

You will hear people talking in eight different situations.
For questions **1–8**, choose the best answer, **A**, **B** or **C**.

1   You hear two people talking in a hotel.
    What is the relationship between them?

    A   They are both staying at the hotel.

    B   They are both attending the same conference.

    C   They are both in the same party of tourists.

2   You hear someone talking on the telephone.
    What is she doing?

    A   demanding an apology

    B   insisting on an action

    C   asking for a favour

3   You hear an advertisement for a magazine.
    What does this month's issue have that's unusual?

    A   an extra part

    B   a special interview

    C   a competition

4   You hear someone talking about a job interview.
    How does she feel?

    A   She is looking forward to the interview.

    B   She is confident of being offered the job.

    C   She is not very interested in the job.

5   You hear someone talking on the telephone.
    Why won't he go to the party?

    A   He feels ill.

    B   He has to do something else.

    C   He doesn't want to go.

6   You hear two people talking in a café.
    What is their opinion of their trip?

    A   It cost too much.

    B   It is badly organized.

    C   The places they visit are boring.

7   You receive a telephone call.
    Who's phoning?

    A   a representative of a telephone company

    B   a local journalist

    C   a telephone repair engineer

8   You hear someone talking at a party.
    What is he talking about?

    A   a new TV channel

    B   a new TV programme

    C   a new TV star

PART 2

You will hear part of a radio programme in which postcards are discussed.
For questions **9–18**, complete the sentences.

POSTCARDS

The exhibition has been organized by the   **9** _____ .

The first postcards in Britain were   **10** _____ .

The words and pictures on the first picture postcards were

11 _____ .

In 1902 postcards were allowed to have a   **12** _____ .

In those days a lot of postcards were kept in   **13** _____ .

At that time the postal service was   **14** _____ .

One reason why people stopped using postcards so much was that

15 _____ went up.

The only postcards collected in the 1950s were funny or showed

16 _____ .

Postcards showing street scenes have   **17** _____ .

In the early 20th Century postcards were a kind of   **18** _____ .

PART 3

You will hear five different people talking about a famous sportsman who has retired.
For questions **19–23**, choose from the list **A–F** who each speaker is. Use the letters only once. There is one extra letter which you do not need to use.

A a sports official

B a teacher
Speaker 1 19

Speaker 2 20

C a player
Speaker 3 21

D a fan
Speaker 4 22

E a childhood friend
Speaker 5 23

F a journalist

PART 4

You will hear part of a radio programme about people's jobs.
For questions **24–30**, choose the best answer **A, B** or **C**.

24   Nick decided to work in his present job

    A   when he started his tourism course.

    B   because he didn't enjoy being an
        accountant.

    C   while he was still doing a course.

25   To get a job as a Tour Leader with High
    Adventure Holidays, you have to

    A   have experience of travel.

    B   be good at dealing with people.

    C   know a lot about other countries.

26   We are told that, when leading a tour, Tour
    Leaders have to be able to

    A   deal with demanding people.

    B   react to problems calmly.

    C   forget their own wishes.

27   Adventure holiday tour leaders are different
    from other tour leaders because

    A   they don't have any time on their own.

    B   they have to travel longer distances.

    C   they have to follow strict instructions.

28   According to Nick, a big disadvantage of the
    job is that he

    A   can't talk about his own problems.

    B   often has to change arrangements.

    C   may not like members of the group.

29   What does Nick say about tour leaders'
    careers?

    A   Leaders go to more interesting places
        after a while.

    B   Leaders' salaries tend to be low at first.

    C   Most tour leaders eventually do office-
        based jobs.

30   What does Nick particularly like about the
    job?

    A   remembering the places he has been to

    B   being appreciated by others

    C   making friends that he keeps

Paper 5 Speaking (15 minutes for 2 candidates)

PART 1

(about 4 minutes)

Practise answering these questions.

Have you travelled a lot?
Which countries have you been to?
Would you like to study in an English-speaking country? OR How long have you been studying in Britain?
When did you start learning English?
Do you go to lessons full-time or part-time now?

PART 2

(about 4 minutes)

Both candidates should look at pictures 5A and 5B on page 127.

The pictures show two popular sports.

Candidate A

Compare and contrast these pictures, saying how you feel about these sports. You have about a minute to do this.

Candidate B

Talk about which of these sports you would prefer to do. You have about 20 seconds to do this.

Both candidates should now look at pictures 5C and 5D on page 127.

The pictures show people enjoying different types of music.

Candidate B

Compare and contrast these pictures, saying which kind of music you prefer listening to, and why. You have about a minute to do this.

Candidate A

Talk about which of these kinds of music you prefer. You have about 20 seconds to do this.

PART 3

(about 3 minutes)

Both candidates should look at pictures 5E–5J on page 128.

The pictures show people in different jobs. A friend of yours is going to leave school soon with good exam results. He or she wants to have a career which will give job satisfaction and the chance to earn a good salary.

Talk to each other and decide which would be the **three** most suitable careers for your friend and which, if any, would be unsuitable.

PART 4

(about 4 minutes)

Now think about these questions. Tell each other what your opinions are.

• What are, or will be, the most important things to you about your career?

• How many hours a day do you think people ought to work?

• Is it possible to have both a family life and a successful career?

• Do you think you would enjoy running your own business? What do you think are the advantages and disadvantages of doing that?

• What sort of person makes a good manager?

CAMBRIDGE
EXAMINATIONS, CERTIFICATES AND DIPLOMAS
ENGLISH AS A FOREIGN LANGUAGE

University of Cambridge
Local Examinations Syndicate
International   Examinations

For Supervisor's use only

Shade here if the candidate is
ABSENT or has WITHDRAWN

➡ ▭ ⬅

Ⓧ

Examination Details	9999/01	99/D99
Examination Title	First Certificate in English	
Centre/Candidate No.	AA999/9999	
Candidate Name	A.N. EXAMPLE	

• Sign here if the details above are correct

SAMPLE

• Tell the Supervisor now if the details above
  are not correct

Candidate Answer Sheet: FCE Paper 1 Reading

Use a pencil

Mark ONE letter for each
question.

For example, if you think **B** is
the right answer to the
question, mark your answer
sheet like this:

0 A B D

Change your answer like
this:

0 A D

6	A B C D E F G H I
7	A B C D E F G H I
8	A B C D E F G H I
9	A B C D E F G H I
10	A B C D E F G H I
11	A B C D E F G H I
12	A B C D E F G H I
13	A B C D E F G H I
14	A B C D E F G H I
15	A B C D E F G H I
16	A B C D E F G H I
17	A B C D E F G H I
18	A B C D E F G H I
19	A B C D E F G H I
20	A B C D E F G H I

21	A B C D E F G H I
22	A B C D E F G H I
23	A B C D E F G H I
24	A B C D E F G H I
25	A B C D E F G H I
26	A B C D E F G H I
27	A B C D E F G H I
28	A B C D E F G H I
29	A B C D E F G H I
30	A B C D E F G H I
31	A B C D E F G H I
32	A B C D E F G H I
33	A B C D E F G H I
34	A B C D E F G H I
35	A B C D E F G H I

1	A B C D E F G H I
2	A B C D E F G H I
3	A B C D E F G H I
4	A B C D E F G H I
5	A B C D E F G H I

© UCLES/K&J.

You may make photocopies of this answer sheet for classroom use (but please note that copyright law does not normally permit multiple copying of published material).

CAMBRIDGE

EXAMINATIONS, CERTIFICATES AND DIPLOMAS
ENGLISH AS A FOREIGN LANGUAGE

University of Cambridge
Local Examinations Syndicate
International   Examinations

For Supervisor's use only

Shade here if the candidate is
ABSENT or has WITHDRAWN

➡ ▭ ⬅

☒

Examination Details	9999/03 99/D99
Examination Title	First Certificate in English
Centre/Candidate No.	AA999/9999
Candidate Name	A.N. EXAMPLE

• Sign here if the details above are correct

SAMPLE

- -

• Tell the Supervisor now if the details above
  are not correct

Candidate Answer Sheet: FCE Paper 3 Use of English

Use a pencil

For **Part 1**: Mark ONE letter for each question.

For example, if you think **C** is the
right answer to the question,
mark your answer sheet like this:

0	A B C D

For **Parts 2, 3, 4** and **5**: Write your
answers in the spaces next to the
numbers like this:

0	example

Part 1				
1	A	B	C	D
2	A	B	C	D
3	A	B	C	D
4	A	B	C	D
5	A	B	C	D
6	A	B	C	D
7	A	B	C	D
8	A	B	C	D
9	A	B	C	D
10	A	B	C	D
11	A	B	C	D
12	A	B	C	D
13	A	B	C	D
14	A	B	C	D
15	A	B	C	D

Part 2	Do not write here
16	16
17	17
18	18
19	19
20	20
21	21
22	22
23	23
24	24
25	25
26	26
27	27
28	28
29	29
30	30

Turn
over
for
Parts
3 - 5
➡

© UCLES/K&J.

Part 3

		Do not write here		
31		31 0	1	2
32		32 0	1	2
33		33 0	1	2
34		34 0	1	2
35		35 0	1	2
36		36 0	1	2
37		37 0	1	2
38		38 0	1	2
39		39 0	1	2
40		40 0	1	2

Part 4

		Do not write here
41		41
42		42
43		43
44		44
45		45
46		46
47		47
48		48
49		49
50		50
51		51
52		52
53		53
54		54
55		55

Part 5

		Do not write here
56		56
57		57
58		58
59		59
60		60
61		61
62		62
63		63
64		64
65		65

SAMPLE

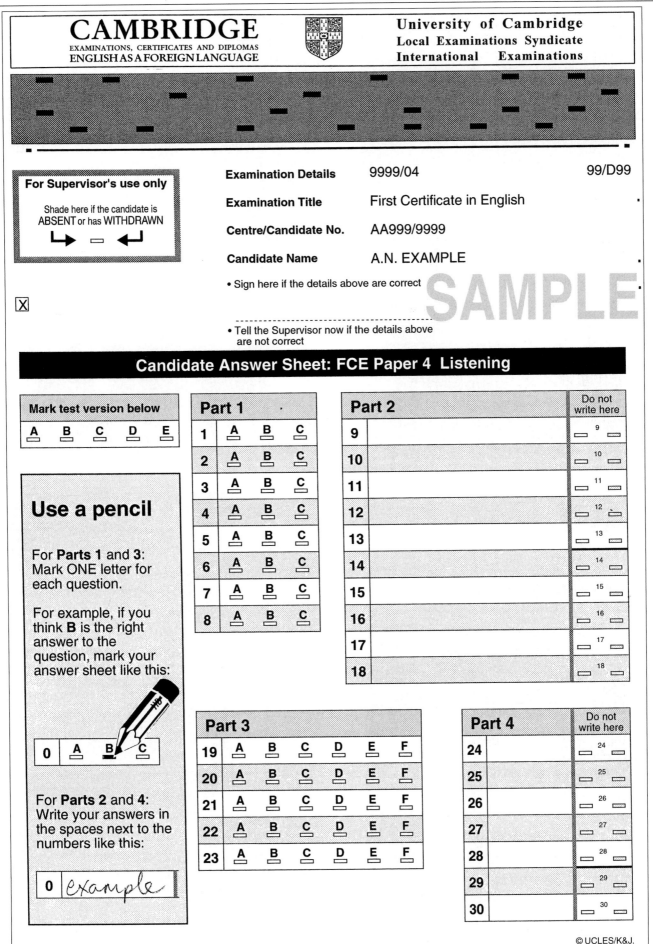

CAMBRIDGE
EXAMINATIONS, CERTIFICATES AND DIPLOMAS
ENGLISH AS A FOREIGN LANGUAGE

University of Cambridge
Local Examinations Syndicate
International Examinations

For Supervisor's use only

Shade here if the candidate is
ABSENT or has WITHDRAWN

X

Examination Details	9999/04	99/D99
Examination Title	First Certificate in English	
Centre/Candidate No.	AA999/9999	
Candidate Name	A.N. EXAMPLE	

• Sign here if the details above are correct

SAMPLE

• Tell the Supervisor now if the details above
are not correct

Candidate Answer Sheet: FCE Paper 4 Listening

Mark test version below

A B C D E

Use a pencil

For **Parts 1** and **3**:
Mark ONE letter for
each question.

For example, if you
think **B** is the right
answer to the
question, mark your
answer sheet like this:

| 0 | A | B | C |

For **Parts 2** and **4**:
Write your answers in
the spaces next to the
numbers like this:

| 0 | example |

Part 1

1	A	B	C
2	A	B	C
3	A	B	C
4	A	B	C
5	A	B	C
6	A	B	C
7	A	B	C
8	A	B	C

Part 2 — Do not write here

9		9
10		10
11		11
12		12
13		13
14		14
15		15
16		16
17		17
18		18

Part 3

19	A	B	C	D	E	F
20	A	B	C	D	E	F
21	A	B	C	D	E	F
22	A	B	C	D	E	F
23	A	B	C	D	E	F

Part 4 — Do not write here

24		24
25		25
26		26
27		27
28		28
29		29
30		30

© UCLES/K&J.

1A

1B

1C

1D

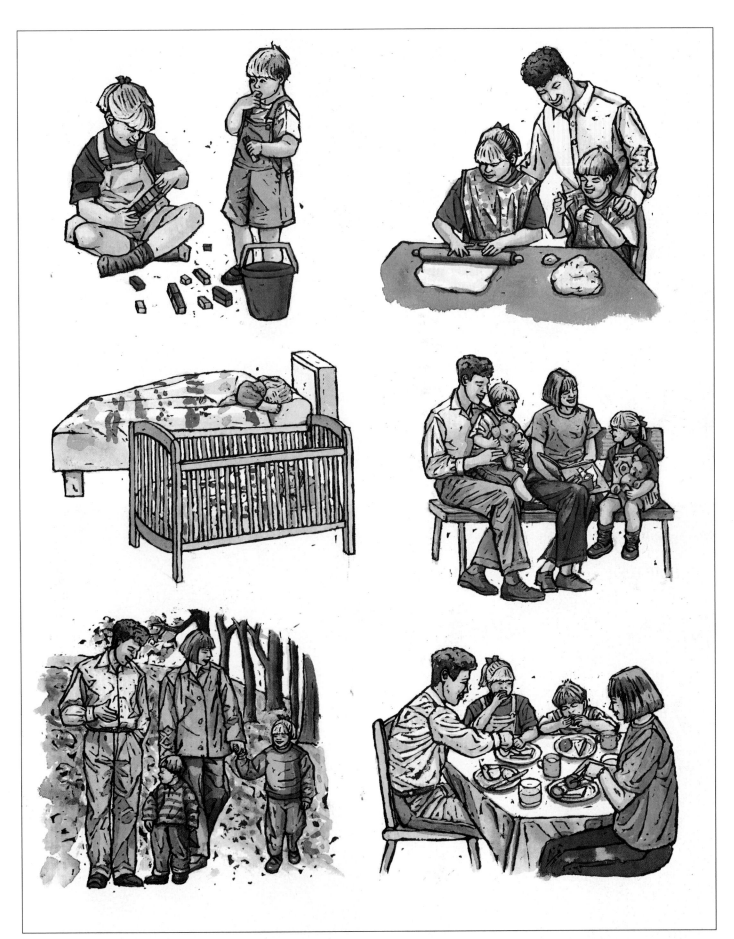

2A

2B

2C

2D

3A

3B

3D

3C

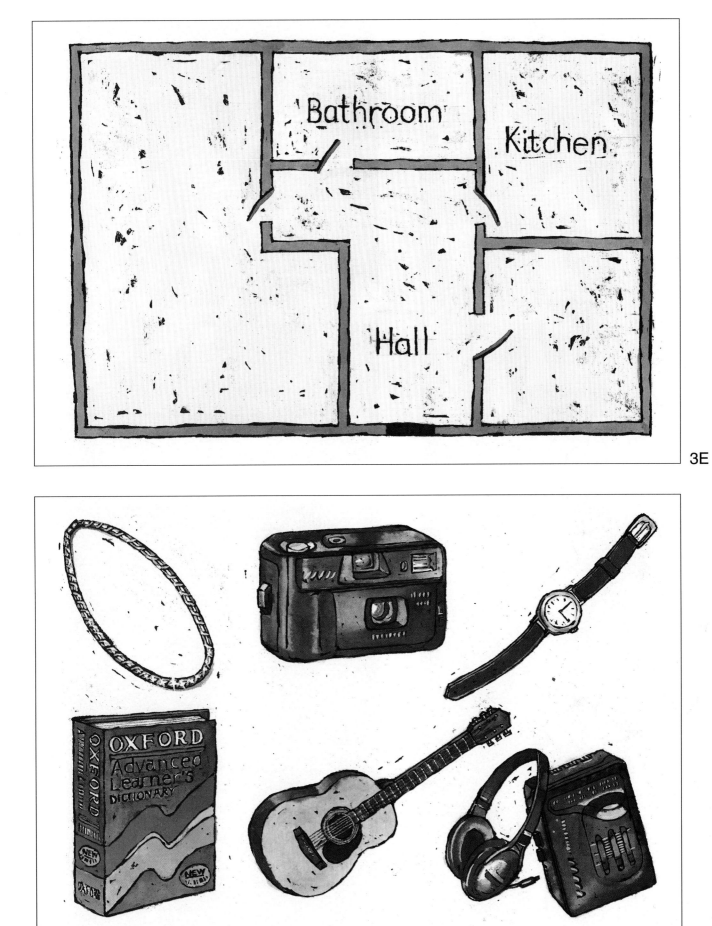

3E

4E

4A

4B

4C

4D

5B

5D

5A

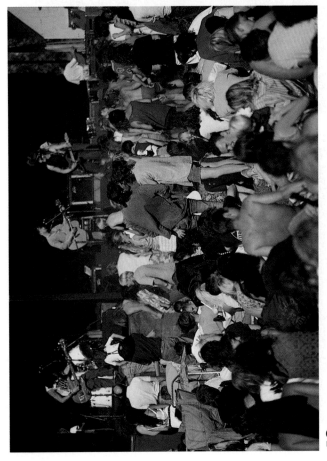

5C

127

5E

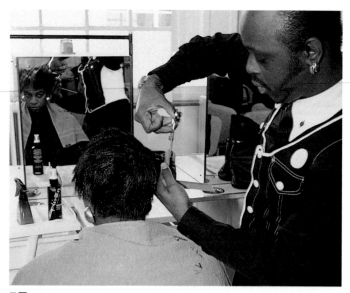

5F

5G

5H

5I

5J

Key

Paper 1

PART 1
1 D	3 G	5 F
2 A	4 B	6 C

PART 2
7 C	10 A	13 B
8 C	11 A	14 D
9 A	12 B	

PART 3
15 F	18 H	20 B
16 D	19 A	21 E
17 G		

PART 4
22/23	A/C (any order)	30	C
24	B	31	D
25/26	B/D (any order)	32	C
27/28	C/E (any order)	33/34	A/D (any order)
29	A	35	E

Paper 2

PART 1
The UCLES General Mark Scheme for Paper 2 is reproduced on page 139. There are two sample student answers on page 140.

Question 1

CONTENT
The letter should say who is writing and give some personal information. Relevant experience and reasons for wanting the job should be stated. All five questions should be asked.

RANGE
Suitable language to describe personal experience and qualities. Some use of conditional structures would be appropriate. A variety of ways of asking questions should be used.

ORGANIZATION AND COHESION
Letter format, but no addresses need be included. Some paragraphing essential, for example an introductory paragraph about the writer and a paragraph covering the questions that need to be asked.

REGISTER
Formal, but could be fairly friendly in tone.

TARGET READER
Should have a clear picture of the writer and be able to answer the questions.

PART 2
Descriptions of suitable answers for Questions 2, 3 and 4 are given below. Because of the specific nature of the background reading texts, no description is given for Question 5.

Question 2

CONTENT
The article should cover different ideas and tips on dressing in an interesting way, with specific examples as appropriate. There must be some reference to the low cost involved.

RANGE
Language needs to deal with description and opinion, and possibly instructions on how to make things or where to buy them. A good range of vocabulary can be used, for example different adjectives to describe appearance and cost.

ORGANIZATION AND COHESION
There should be an opening paragraph outlining the content of the article. An appropriate title would be useful. The article should come to a definite conclusion.

REGISTER
As the article will appear in a magazine for students, the register can be informal and the whole tone of the article fairly light-hearted.

TARGET READER
Should feel both informed and interested, and possibly entertained.

Question 3

CONTENT
A detailed description of a family celebration. It should be clear what kind of occasion was being celebrated and what form the celebration took.

RANGE
Language used should cover description and narrative, using past tenses. There should be some variety in the expressions used to describe memories and a range of vocabulary, including good use of adjectives.

ORGANIZATION AND COHESION
Letter format, but addresses do not need to be included. Some introductory greetings should be followed by one or two paragraphs about the celebration itself, and a concluding paragraph.

REGISTER
Informal, with appropriate opening and closing phrases.

TARGET READER
Should have a good idea of what took place at the celebration and find the description of it interesting.

Question 4

CONTENT
A suitable story, beginning with the sentence supplied.

RANGE
Past tense narrative should be used, possibly with some language of comparison to describe different situations before and after the arrival of the letter. Expressions should convey some enthusiasm or urgency as appropriate to the story.

ORGANIZATION AND COHESION
There should be some paragraphing and good use of linking devices to structure the sequence of events. There should be a definite ending to the story.

REGISTER
Neutral or fairly informal.

TARGET READER
Should be engaged by the story and interested in finding out what happens.

Paper 3

PART 1

1 A	6 D	11 A
2 C	7 B	12 B
3 D	8 C	13 D
4 B	9 A	14 C
5 D	10 B	15 B

PART 2

16 is/remains	21 as	26 to
17 to/towards	22 There	27 in
18 this/that	23 not	28 by
19 it	24 that/which	29 have
20 of	25 and	30 both

PART 3

There are two marks per question: one mark for each part, as shown below.

31	take (us)	at least
32	even though	I knew
33	have a word	with Jack
34	it didn't/did not matter	to
35	you look after	them (carefully)
36	lie (that) you've/you have	told
37	have a good time/ have good fun	at
38	it reminds me	of
39	better at	describing people than
40	ought to	have thought

PART 4

41 up	46 after	51 for
42 ✓	47 ✓	52 ✓
43 the	48 much	53 about
44 it	49 to	54 ✓
45 at	50 one	55 so

PART 5

56 enables	61 judgement/judgment
57 breathing	62 incorrectly
58 consideration	63 demanding
59 harmful	64 steadily
60 importance	65 difference

Paper 4

PART 1

1 C	4 A	7 A
2 B	5 A	8 C
3 B	6 B	

PART 2

9 over/more than 150
10 information assistant
11 a (small) town
12 was asleep/sleeping
13 luggage/clothes/luggage or clothes
14 Travel Care
15 Terminal Duty Team
16 check-in area
17 Passenger Services
18 flight delays

PART 3

19 E	21 D	23 B
20 A	22 F	

PART 4

24 B	27 A	30 A
25 B	28 A	
26 B	29 C	

Test 2

Paper 1

PART 1

1 G	3 E	5 D
2 C	4 A	6 F

PART 2

7 B	10 A	13 A
8 C	11 B	14 D
9 A	12 D	

PART 3

15 B	17 A	19 E
16 F	18 G	20 C

PART 4

21 A	26 A	31 D
22 D	27 C	32 B
23 C	28 C	33 B
24 B	29 A	34 C
25 C	30 A	35 B

Paper 2

PART 1

There are two sample student answers on page 141.

Question 1

CONTENT
The letter should say whether it is possible to meet Jo at the airport. If not, some suggestions about how to get to the writer's home would be useful. At least two of the suggested presents illustrated should be referred to in detail and reasons for suggesting them may be included. There should be some expression of positive feelings about Jo's visit.

RANGE
Language used should cover description and making suggestions. There should be some variety in the vocabulary used to describe the presents. Some different expressions of enthusiasm and/or welcome could be included.

ORGANIZATION AND COHESION
Letter format, but addresses need not be included.

REGISTER
Informal and friendly in tone.

TARGET READER
Should get a clear idea of what presents to buy and feel excited about the visit.

PART 2

Question 2

CONTENT
The letter of application should give details of who is writing and why they would be suitable for the job, including any experience of working with children. There should be at least two specific examples of activities the writer could offer to run.

RANGE
Language used should cover personal details and descriptions of activities. There should be a range of vocabulary related to job applications and working with children.

ORGANIZATION AND COHESION
Letter format, but addresses need not be included.

REGISTER
Formal.

TARGET READER
Should get a good picture of the applicant and know whether or not he or she would be suitable.

Question 3

CONTENT
The account should be related to one specific occasion and be sufficiently detailed to convey what kind of event it was and what it was like to attend it. Some sense of enthusiasm should be conveyed.

RANGE
Language should cover description and personal opinion. Vocabulary relevant to the chosen event should be used.

ORGANIZATION AND COHESION
An opening paragraph should specify the event. There should be suitable paragraphing and a strong ending.

REGISTER
Semi-formal or informal, provided that the register is consistent throughout.

TARGET READER
Should gain a distinct impression of the event and be interested in the account.

Question 4

CONTENT
The article should give the writer's opinion on the question asked and include suitable examples to reinforce the argument.

RANGE
The language of opinion should be used to present the writer's own views. There should be some topic vocabulary specifically related to television and to children's lifestyles.

ORGANIZATION AND COHESION
There should be an opening paragraph outlining the content of the article. An appropriate title would be useful. The article should come to a definite conclusion.

REGISTER
Neutral or semi-formal.

TARGET READER
Should fully understand the writer's opinions and the reasoning behind them.

Paper 3

PART 1

1 C	6 B	11 D
2 D	7 B	12 C
3 A	8 B	13 A
4 B	9 D	14 A
5 D	10 A	15 C

PART 2

16 in	24 become/got/been
17 the	25 of
18 give	26 for
19 to	27 or
20 than	28 which
21 An	29 being/getting
22 great/good	30 because
23 last/past	

PART 3

There are two marks per question: one mark for each part, as shown below.

31	have made	(some) improvements to/in
32	didn't/did not have lacked	enough/the courage OR the courage
33	had/found no difficulty/ problem(s)/trouble	(in) getting
34	as if/though	he was enjoying
35	doubt (whether/if/that)	they live/they're living/ they are living
36	wasn't/was not	in favour of
37	she didn't/did not/ wouldn't/would not mind	working
38	if you'd/you had	gone
39	there was saw	a rise in OR a rise in
40	wasn't/was not used to	making/giving

PART 4

41 of	46 too	51 in
42 ✓	47 so	52 including
43 they	48 the	53 as
44 a	49 ✓	54 themselves
45 ✓	50 for	55 there

PART 5

56 possibility	61 surprisingly
57 defence/defense (US)	62 reputation
58 inaccurate	63 motorists
59 reliable	64 choice
60 successful	65 vary

Paper 4

PART 1

1 B	4 A	7 C
2 A	5 B	8 B
3 C	6 B	

PART 2

9 up to/no more than/not over/a maximum of 4/four minutes
10 special nature
11 (a) separate microphone
12 (the) best interview
13 issues
14 (any) equipment
15 (a) special project/special projects
16 Our Society Today
17 clearly labelled/labelled clearly
18 for collection

PART 3

19 D	21 E	23 A
20 F	22 C	

PART 4

24 Y	27 N	30 Y
25 N	28 Y	
26 Y	29 Y	

Test 3

Paper 1

PART 1
1 D	4 A	7 B
2 F	5 G	
3 H	6 E	

PART 2
8 A	11 B	14 B
9 B	12 A	15 D
10 D	13 D	

PART 3
16 F	18 D	20 A
17 C	19 B	21 E

PART 4
22	D	29	E
23	B	30	B
24	A	31	C
25	E	32/33	A/C (any order)
26	C	34	C
27	C	35	D
28	B		

Paper 2

PART 1
There are two sample student answers on page 142.

Question 1

CONTENT
The letter should ask the three questions indicated and give advice to the friend, covering the suggestions listed.

RANGE
A variety of ways of making suggestions could be used. There should be some topic vocabulary relevant to studying and college life.

ORGANIZATION AND COHESION
Letter format, but addresses need not be included. There should be some introductory greeting and the final sentences should confirm the main message.

REGISTER
Informal.

TARGET READER
Should feel reassured and be able to act on the advice given.

PART 2

Question 2

CONTENT
The report should deal with **one** film in detail, explaining why it would be suitable for use in class. The film must be in English, but may be in any variety of the language, for example American English or Australian English.

RANGE
Language used should cover description, opinion and recommendation. There should be some vocabulary and expressions relevant to learning English.

ORGANIZATION AND COHESION
Report format, with an early mention of the film by name. There should be suitable paragraphing and a separate conclusion.

REGISTER
Informal or semi-formal.

TARGET READER
Should have a detailed impression of the film and be able to decide whether it would be suitable for the class.

Question 3

CONTENT
Suitable story, beginning with the sentence supplied.

RANGE
Past tense narrative should be used. Expressions should convey some urgency or feelings appropriate to the story.

ORGANIZATION AND COHESION
There should be some paragraphing and good use of linking devices to structure the sequence of events. There should be a definite ending to the story.

REGISTER
Neutral or fairly informal.

TARGET READER
Should be engaged by the story and interested in finding out what happened.

Question 4

CONTENT
The letter of application should give details about who is writing and why he or she would be a suitable applicant for the job. Some reference should be made to the expected age-group of the tourists and there should be some specific examples of places the tourists could be taken to visit.

RANGE
Language used should cover giving personal information and also information about and descriptions of places. There should be a range of vocabulary suitable to applications and to tourism.

ORGANIZATION AND COHESION
Letter format, but addresses need not be included.

REGISTER
Formal.

TARGET READER
Should get a clear picture of the applicant and be able to decide whether he or she would be suitable.

Paper 3

PART 1

1 B	6 C	11 B
2 B	7 C	12 B
3 A	8 C	13 A
4 A	9 D	14 A
5 D	10 D	15 B

PART 2

16 with/in	21 into	26 in
17 more	22 a	27 until/till
18 let	23 their	28 whose
19 whatever	24 for	29 are
20 to	25 when/where	30 many

PART 3

There are two marks per question: one mark for each part, as shown below.

31	she may not	have understood
32	had/got	our car repaired
33	(that) I (should)	take it
34	gave me	such confusing information
35	no point	(in) worrying
36	I'd/I would rather	not sit
37	wished me	a pleasant journey
38	turned down	my offer
39	instead of going	on
40	had/took a look	at

PART 4

41 get	46 did	51 them
42 ✓	47 herself	52 ✓
43 as	48 and	53 yet
44 it	49 time	54 ✓
45 of	50 ✓	55 for

PART 5

56 extraordinary	61 daily
57 excitement	62 sale
58 throughout	63 upsetting
59 worldwide	64 harmless
60 imagination	65 enjoyment

Paper 4

PART 1

1 A	4 B	7 A
2 B	5 C	8 A
3 A	6 A	

PART 2

9 shops (too) crowded
10 children's area
11 not enough signs
12 comfortable seating
13 (big/wide) range of food
14 horrible design
15 (the) bargains/low prices in (the) shops
16 (lots of/endless/long/big) queues
17 (the) fun room
18 poor quality (of/of the) food

PART 3

19 A	21 E	23 F
20 D	22 B	

PART 4

24 C	27 A	30 C
25 B	28 C	
26 A	29 A	

Test 4

Paper 1

PART 1

1 F	4 H	6 B
2 C	5 A	7 G
3 D		

PART 2

8 A	11 A	14 C
9 B	12 D	15 B
10 C	13 D	

PART 3

16 B	19 C	22 D
17 E	20 A	
18 G	21 F	

PART 4

23	A	31	C
24/25	B/E (any order)	32	A
26	A	33	A
27/28	B/E (any order)	34	C
29	A	35	C
30	D		

Paper 2

PART 1

There are two sample student answers on page 143.

Question 1

CONTENT
The letter of complaint should give precise details of the problem and ask for some form of compensation. Specific information should be given about when and where the holiday took place.

RANGE
Past tenses should be used to refer to what happened. There should be some sense of indignation and expressions that request further action.

ORGANIZATION AND COHESION
Letter format, but addresses need not be included. Cohesive devices should be used to link what happened to the complaint.

REGISTER
Formal.

TARGET READER
Should be fully informed and be persuaded to take the action requested.

PART 2

Question 2

CONTENT
The letter should give detailed information about the place and the weather, as well as advice on what to include in the one small bag to be carried.

RANGE
Description and opinion should both be present. There should be some topic vocabulary relevant to walking holidays.

ORGANIZATION AND COHESION
Letter format, but addresses need not be included. There should be some introductory greeting and a final expression of good wishes for the holiday.

REGISTER
Informal and friendly in tone.

TARGET READER
Should be pleased to receive the letter and be able to act on the advice given.

Question 3

CONTENT
The composition should make it clear whether the writer agrees or disagrees with the statement and suitable reasons should be given to support the argument.

RANGE
Language of opinion and description should be used. There should be some topic vocabulary relevant to free time activities.

ORGANIZATION AND COHESION
The composition should be clearly organized, with an introduction stating the writer's point of view, suitable paragraphs expanding on it and a conclusion in the final paragraph.

REGISTER
Semi-formal.

TARGET READER
Should have a clear idea of the writer's point of view and be able to use the information in research.

Question 4

CONTENT
The report should cover a range of evening activities suitable for people of the same sort of age as the writer, with any practical details such as location and cost included. At least two suggestions should be made.

RANGE
Language used should cover description and personal opinion. Topic vocabulary relevant to evening activities should be included.

ORGANIZATION AND COHESION
Report format, possibly with sub-headings. There should be a brief introduction to the report and a conclusion.

REGISTER
Formal.

TARGET READER
Should be fully informed about appropriate activities and know what to organize.

Paper 3

PART 1

1 D	6 B	11 A
2 B	7 A	12 B
3 A	8 D	13 C
4 B	9 A	14 A
5 C	10 D	15 C

PART 2

16 as	21 other	26 to
17 all	22 a	27 have/need
18 way	23 how/what	28 be
19 or	24 remind	29 where
20 are	25 something	30 such

PART 3

There are two marks per question: one mark for each part, as shown below.

31	there was something something was/ had gone/was going	wrong with OR wrong with
32	was prevented	from going
33	no-one/no one/ nobody else	apart from/except (for)/but (for)/other than
34	the entire day	watching
35	will have to	be paid
36	passed (by)/gone by	before I saw
37	she objects to	doing
38	of Jeremy to	make up
39	him of	taking part in
40	too much pride	to admit

PART 4

41	✓	46	neither	51	at
42	highly	47	time	52	✓
43	of	48	love	53	either
44	like	49	✓	54	that
45	as	50	they	55	for

PART 5

56	comparatively	61	skilled/skil(l)ful
57	medical	62	suspicious
58	contribution	63	professionally
59	advice	64	illegal
60	injuries	65	equality

Paper 4

PART 1

1	B	4	C	7	B
2	B	5	B	8	C
3	B	6	B		

PART 2

9 Theatre Studies
10 practical
11 Drama in Education
12 Artistic Managers
13 financial situation
14 good reviews
15 best comedy production
16 (a) TV commercial/advert/advertisement
17 (a) major/large/big/(an) important company
18 to be unemployed

PART 3

19	E	22	B	21	D
20	F	23	A		

PART 4

24	N	27	A	29	D
25	A	28	D	30	A
26	D				

Test 5

Paper 1

PART 1

1	B	3	F	5	G
2	D	4	A	6	E

PART 2

7	C	10	A	12	C
8	C	11	B	13	A
9	D				

PART 3

14	G	17	A	19	H
15	B	18	F	20	C
16	D				

PART 4

21	A	26	D	31	E
22	A	27	A	32	A
23	B	28	E	33	E
24	A	29	B	34	E
25	C	30	C	35	B

Paper 2

PART 1

There are two sample student answers on page 144.

Question 1

CONTENT
The letter should contain a polite enquiry as to whether it is possible to change arrangements, explaining why this is necessary. Precise details of the course and the timing of arrival should be included.

RANGE
Language used should give information and make a polite request. There should be some topic vocabulary relevant to the course.

ORGANIZATION AND COHESION
Letter format, but addresses need not be included.

REGISTER
Formal.

TARGET READER
Should know what the writer's plans are, understand the reason for the changes in plans, and be able to decide what further action to take.

Question 2

CONTENT
The article should refer to **one** town or city, giving information about a reasonable selection of sights to see within a single day.

RANGE
Language used should cover description and include some expressions of advice. Topic vocabulary should be relevant to towns and cities.

ORGANIZATION AND COHESION
There should be an early mention of which town or city is being referred to. The article should be suitably paragraphed.

REGISTER
Neutral.

TARGET READER
Should be fully informed and be able to plan a day's visit.

Question 3

CONTENT
The composition should say whether the writer agrees or disagrees with the statement and the argument should be supported with suitable examples.

RANGE
Language used should convey opinion and description. There should be some topic vocabulary relevant to the environment.

ORGANIZATION AND COHESION
The composition should be clearly organized, with an introduction stating the writer's point of view, suitable paragraphs expanding on it and a conclusion in the final paragraph.

REGISTER
Neutral or semi-formal.

TARGET READER
Should be able to form a clear idea of the writer's point of view.

Question 4

CONTENT

The account should cover the writer's memories of his or her first day at school in an interesting way.

RANGE
Past tenses should be used to describe the day and the writer's feelings should be described with suitable expressions.

ORGANIZATION AND COHESION
The account should be suitably paragraphed and come to a definite conclusion.

REGISTER
Neutral or semi-formal.

TARGET READER
Should be informed and interested.

Paper 3

PART 1

1 B	6 A	11 A
2 B	7 B	12 B
3 D	8 C	13 D
4 D	9 C	14 A
5 B	10 B	15 B

PART 2

16 taken	24 it
17 to	25 is
18 as	26 by/through
19 of	27 been
20 no	28 for/in
21 and	29 Because/As/Since
22 do	30 well
23 unless	

PART 3

There are two marks per question: one mark for each part, as shown below.

31	better	apologize to
32	are unlikely to	have received
33	got/had the impression	(that) something
34	with	so much skill
35	the reason for	his change
36	are we supposed	to pick
37	him not to	repeat to
38	my surprise(,)	it turned out
39	give her	the/an opportunity to OR
	give her	the/a chance to
40	there are	hardly any tickets OR
	hardly any tickets	are

PART 4

41 ✓	46 by	51 possible
42 a	47 it	52 in
43 as	48 one	53 ✓
44 for	49 ✓	54 that
45 of	50 ✓	55 do

PART 5

56 delightful	60 attractive	63 shortage
57 unchanged	61 crowded	64 traditional
58 commercial	62 fame	65 enjoyable
59 charming		

Paper 4

PART 1

1 B	4 A	7 A
2 B	5 B	8 A
3 A	6 B	

PART 2

9 Postcard Traders Association
10 blank
11 on the same side
12 divided back
13 albums
14 quick and reliable
15 postage rates
16 countryside views
17 historical value
18 news reporting

PART 3

19 D	22 F
20 C	23 B
21 A	

PART 4

24 C	27 A	29 A
25 B	28 A	30 B
26 C		

Paper 2 General Mark Scheme

UNIVERSITY OF CAMBRIDGE LOCAL EXAMINATIONS SYNDICATE

REVISED FCE 2 - GENERAL MARK SCHEME - JUNE 1995

Band 5	• Good range of structure and vocabulary within the task set (a) • Minimal errors of structure, vocabulary, spelling and punctuation • Points covered as required with evidence of original output • Text suitably set out and ideas clearly linked (b) • Register appropriate to task and sustained (c) ∴ Very positive effect on target reader
Band 4	• Good range of structure and vocabulary within the task set but text not always fluent • Errors only when more complex vocabulary/structure attempted; spelling and punctuation generally accurate • Points covered as required with sufficient detail • Text suitably set out and ideas clearly linked (b) • Register appropriate to the task and sustained (c) ∴ Positive effect on target reader
Band 3	• An adequate range of structure and vocabulary to fulfil the requirements of the task • Some errors which do not impede communication • Points covered but some non-essential details omitted • Text suitably set out and ideas clearly linked; linking devices fairly simple • Register on the whole appropriate to the task ∴ Satisfactory effect on target reader
Band 2	• Range of structure and vocabulary too limited to meet all requirements of the task • Errors sometimes obscure communication/distract the reader • Some omissions or large amount of lifting/irrelevant material • Text not clearly laid out; linking devices rarely used • Some attempt at appropriate register but no consistency ∴ Message not clearly communicated to target reader
Band 1	• Range of structure and vocabulary very narrow • No evidence of any systematic control of language • Notable omissions in coverage of points needed and/or considerable irrelevance • Poor organization of text; lack of linking • No awareness of appropriacy of register ∴ A very negative effect on target reader
Band 0	Too little language for assessment (fewer than 50 words) or totally irrelevant or totally illegible (d)

Notes:

(a) Task achievement entails completing the task within the word limits.

(b) Conventions of paragraphing, letter format, etc., expected here, with cohesion maintained as appropriate for FCE level; additional notes for specific tasks are provided for examiners.

(c) Fine-tuning of register is not expected at this level but some distinction between semi-formal (neutral) and informal needs to be demonstrated and **sustained** to fit into Bands 4 and 5.

(d) Poor handwriting is penalized.

Sample Student Answers

(Paper 2 Part 1)

The following pieces of writing are genuine student answers and are therefore not flawless; they are examples of at least a pass level at FCE.

Test 1

01/12/94

Dear Mrs Malone,

My name is Kristin. I'm 20 years old and I come from Germany. I found your advertisement in the magazine and I'm very interested in helping you.

I'm studying English and that's why the holiday could help me to practise your language. Furthermore I like children and Scotland as well. By the way, I spent one year as an au-pair in London in 1994. I'm keen on nearly all activities in the open air.

But let me ask a few questions, please. I need to know when exactly you plan to go on holiday. How old are your children? Please, could you tell me, too what kind of help do you expect and how many hours a day for. And what about the payment? What do you suggest?

I'm looking forward to hearing from you and I hope I can help you and you me.

Yours faithfully

Kristin Holze

Dear Mrs Malone,

I am writting from France, where I have read your advertisement regarding a three-week summer holiday in an English-language magazine. Despite the fact that I am only eighteen, I am energetic and very sociable. I am all the more enticed by your advertisement that I both need to improve my English and am fond of children.

However, there are a few details I would like to know in order to avoid any misunderstanding.

First of all, since I would like to have enough time to visit such a beautiful country, I need to know how many hours a day do you need some help and what kind of help do you expect.

Furthermore, as I do not feel capable of looking after babies under two years old owing to my lack of experience, I would like you to inform me on their ages.

I would appreciate if you could let me know as well the dates when you want me to come. Moreover, I wonder if whether I will be given a wage or I will be put up only.

I am really looking forward to receive a letter from you.

Yours sincerly

Gilles Barbe

Test 2

5th March

Dear Jo,

Thank you for your letter. I'm glad to hear you'll come soon. I'm so sorry, but I have an appointment at 15.30, so I won't be able to meet you at the airport. Can I meet you at the railway station?

By the way, you want to know about presents, don't you? I'll suggest you some presents. I think the best thing is a CD. My parents love music specially opera and they are interested in the music from the Sydney Opera House. If you give them this CD, they'll be glad, I'm sure.

One more thing I can suggest you is a book. Last week when I went to a book shop, I found quite nice book. The title is 'Beautiful Australia', which includes 50 colour photographs. If you bring it, you can explain about the sceneries in Australia and also we can enjoy looking it. We want to know well about Australia.

We're looking forward to meeting you soon. Anyway, ring me to arrange our meeting time.

Love,

Hiromi

Dear Jo,

Thank's for your lovely letter.

I am very pleased hearing that you will be here in England on March 14th.

It has been two years since met for the last time. I really miss you and also my family.

And off course I will pick you up at the airport by the time you have arrived. You can rely on me. I will be there on time. I used to do that, didn't I?

By the way, about some present that you will give us. Why don't you bring some thing like T-shirt with particular Australian design or toy kangaroos which is a very popular animal in Australia. We will be very glad having some presents from you. The point is, you can spend your time here with us. Don't forget to call me one day before you arrived.

I'm looking forward to hearing from you.

Yours,

Dhani

Test 3

London, 22th November 1994

Dear Peter,

I received your kind letter last week and I was surprised of how depressed you are. I know that the first term at college is very hard because when I started my college, one year ago, was the same for me. Even though you feel exhausted you haven't to give up! I think that you should speak with your teacher trying to look for a solution. Maybe she can help you. Another thing that I think it's very important is that you have to eat complete meals, because when you study you need a lot of energies. If where you live it's too noisy, you could study in the college library or you could look for another flat in a more quiet place. If you need I could lend you some money; you have only to ask me!

In your letter you wrote me that you haven't time to meet other people because you have always to study. I suggest you to go out and try to enjoy yourself. However, don't give up!!! Have you thought about your life without a diploma? It's not easy to find a job without it. Now, I'm sorry I haven't more time and hoping that you'll think a lot of what you are going to do …

See you soon

Patricia

Dear Mary,

Thank you for your letter. I feel sorry for you now, because I know how much you wanted to go to college.

I remember my first term. As you, I thought of giving up. I was so exhausted too, but I didn't. You have to stay at college because you need it if you want a good job later.

Try to have some rest (do you sleep enough? don't you go out too often?) Book your Saturday for your study, you will be more relax. If you have any problem with your lessons, talk to your teachers. They can give you good advice and tell you how to learn easily. If your home is too noisy, try to find another one or, if you can't, go to the college library to study.

You say you've got no money. Why? I know how expensive studying is, but first of all, don't waste your money. Don't go out too often, accept only parties in Saturday night (also because you can sleep on Sunday!). Maybe, you can find a holiday job - ask your Students Club, they might have some good opportunities.

Let me know if you settle in your new life. I wish you the best.

Lots of love

Isabelle.

142

Test 4

Dear Sir,

I am writing to complain about the arrangements your travel company made for me and my friend while we were in London.

According to your advertisement, we could choose whatever we wanted. We wanted to go to a musical. However, only cinema was available.

To make matters worse, the seats were terrible and we couldn't see what was going on on the screen. In your advertisement you had written, 'all you have to do is sit back and enjoy the show!' My experience was bad. You should at least have given us seats so that we could watch the film.

I am very upset at having spent money on this touring holiday, and I would be very pleased if you refunded the money.

I look forward to receiving a reply.

Yours faithfully

Elin Bergseng

Dear Sir/ Madame,

I am writing to complain about the service we had for the four-dAy holiday in London, that we booked with your agency two weeks ago. Although it was clearly written in the brochure, that wwe could see good shows at the theatre, it didn't happen.

In fact there were no tickets available for the theatre, but only for the cinema, which made me very angry. Considering that we didn't have any choice, we went to the cinema, but here the things were not better.

Much to my surpise, we got terrible seats on side at front, but what I most hated about that, was the fact that we couldn't see the screen properly.

As a result, what I am going to ask you, is the refund of money for the tickets of the theatre that my friend and I didn't get because not available - I look forward to hearing from you.

Your faithfully

Biagio Salzillo

Test 5

25th Jun, 1994

Dear Cynthia Canter,

Thank you for your reply dated 24th Jun, 1994 and for your kind arrangement that I can take the full-time course "Holiday English" and stay with a local family. But, I am really sorry to ask if it is possible to change some arrangements.

Can I start my course a day late, i.e. on the 12th of Jul and cancel the booking for accomodation? Just before your letter arrived, my friend who lives in Dublin, informed me that she was going on holiday for two weeks on July 12. If I started my English course on July 12, I could have a day with her. In addition, I can stay in her flat while she is away. I think it is more comfortable and cheeper than staying with a local family.

I am very sorry to make you inconvenient. I would highly appreciate if you help me to start on Jul 12 and to call the accommodation off.

I am looking forward to having your reply as soon as possible.

Yours faithfully,

Mee Kyung, Park

Dear Ms. Canter,

Thank you for your letter. I was glad to learn that you could book a place for me on the course "Holiday English" as well as arrange an accomodation for me.

However, a friend of mine offered me to stay in his flat during my stay in Dublin. So, I would like to know if you could cancel the accomodation you arranged for me.

Furthermore, I would like to inform you that I will arrive at the college only on the morning of July 12 since my friend will be off on holiday for two weeks on this date. Since I haven't seen him for a long time, I would like to spend the Monday 11th July with him. Please, could you let me know if there is any problem in starting the school one day late.

I apologize for the inconvenience caused and look forward to receiving your reply as soon as possible.

Yours sincerely,

Jos Chambordon

Tapescripts

TEST 1

PART 1

You will hear people talking in eight different situations. For questions 1–8, choose the best answer A, B or C.

1   *You are walking in the street when somebody stops you and speaks to you. What does he want you to do?*
  A   give him directions
  B   give him an address
  C   take him somewhere

PAUSE 5 SECONDS

Excuse me, I wonder if you could give me a hand. I'm looking for The National Central Bank and I seem to have got a bit lost. I've got this map here that they sent me and they've marked where it is, but I'm afraid I can't work it out. I keep ending up in the same place. I know it's very near here, so would you mind terribly coming along with me and pointing out the place – as long as it's not out of your way, of course.

PAUSE 2 SECONDS - REPEAT - PAUSE 2 SECONDS

2   *You hear someone talking on a public telephone. Who is she talking to?*
  A   her employer
  B   another employee
  C   a doctor

PAUSE 5 SECONDS

… I think I'm going to be in a bit late today … could you let him know? … no I can't rearrange it … look, it's a firm appointment … no, I know he gets annoyed if anyone's late, but what can I do? … Yes, I know he'll make me work some extra time to make it up … but you know I haven't been feeling well lately so I want to find out what's wrong with me … OK, I'll see you as soon as I can.

PAUSE 2 SECONDS - REPEAT - PAUSE 2 SECONDS

3   *You hear part of a radio news report. Where is the reporter?*
  A   in a conference hall
  B   outside a building
  C   in a hotel

PAUSE 5 SECONDS

Presenter: … and so, it's over to our reporter, David Muir, who's on the spot.

Reporter: Yes, thank you Sue, we're expecting developments any minute now. For the past few days, I've been staying not far from here and people have been gathering on the streets. It looks as if there might be trouble, if they're not satisfied with the results of the talks. The leaders should be coming out very soon, and the moment they come down the steps I'll try to fight my way through the crowd of other reporters on the pavement and get comments from them.

Presenter: OK, David, we'll be back to you as soon as anything happens.

PAUSE 2 SECONDS - REPEAT - PAUSE 2 SECONDS

4   *You hear someone on the radio describing her career. How does she feel?*
  A   content
  B   frustrated
  C   jealous

PAUSE 5 SECONDS

Yes, I've had a very varied career. I've had my successes and my failures and that's the way life goes. All I can say is, I've never known what's going to happen next. I know that many other actors have had more success than me without my talent, and I could let that bother me, but that's not the way I am. I think that I might not have done everything I'm capable of, but worse things can happen to you.

PAUSE 2 SECONDS - REPEAT - PAUSE 2 SECONDS

5   *You hear part of a radio report. Who is speaking?*
  A   a policeman
  B   a motoring expert
  C   a car driver

PAUSE 5 SECONDS

… so many people just don't seem to understand what a weapon a vehicle is. Every holiday time we have the same thing. Every holiday time we give the same warnings, but every holiday time they take no notice. So many drivers are just so careless, and, frankly, stupid. They obviously don't care about driving properly, or they wouldn't behave like they do. Then they wonder why they get involved in accidents! And when they do, we have to deal with the results.

PAUSE 2 SECONDS - REPEAT - PAUSE 2 SECONDS

6   *You hear someone talking on the telephone. What is he doing?*
  A   giving advice
  B   expressing disapproval
  C   trying to persuade

PAUSE 5 SECONDS

Look, I'm not going to go through this again. It's obvious that you never listen to a word I say, so what's the point in discussing it now? You shouldn't have bought that car. I told you enough times, there are plenty of better ones for the money – but now that you have, it's too late to do anything about it. You asked me what I thought and then you took no notice. Look, I can only tell you what I think – if you choose to ignore me, that's up to you.

PAUSE 2 SECONDS - REPEAT - PAUSE 2 SECONDS

7   *You hear two people discussing the local bus service. What's their opinion of it?*
  A   The service is unreliable.
  B   The fares are too high.
  C   The journeys are very slow.

PAUSE 5 SECONDS

Man: What I object to is that the things never come when they're supposed to.

Woman: Yeah, I mean the other day I must have been waiting for three quarters of an hour. They always seem to take ages to come, don't they?

Man: That's if they even turn up at all. I mean, they make this big thing about how you save money if you use them instead of going by car, and I suppose that's true but …

Woman: … yeah, whether it's cheap or not is neither here nor there if you can never be sure whether they're going to turn up or not.

Man: Quite. I don't know why they even bother to print the timetables.

PAUSE 2 SECONDS - REPEAT - PAUSE 2 SECONDS

8   You hear part of an interview with a sportsman. What is the situation?
    A   He has just won a match.
    B   He is about to play.
    C   He has decided to retire.

PAUSE 5 SECONDS

Well, when I became the champion, I thought there was nothing else left for me to achieve, but after a while, when I'd got used to it, I wanted to win again and again. I'd really like to be out there today, because I still think I can beat almost anyone. But, well, I've had my great victories, and you can't ask for more than that. I realize it's time to call it a day, and after all, I can still play for fun.

PAUSE 2 SECONDS - REPEAT - PAUSE 2 SECONDS

That is the end of Part 1. Now turn to Part 2.

PART 2

You will hear part of a radio programme about Gatwick Airport, an airport near London. For questions 9–18, complete the sentences.

You now have 45 seconds in which to look at Part 2.

PAUSE 45 SECONDS

Announcer: Gatwick has grown from a small local airfield to become the sixth largest international airport in the world. Every year, nearly 20 million passengers pass through. 23,000 people work there, employed by more than 150 companies, but the responsibility of dealing directly with the travelling public is in the hands of relatively few men and women. Our reporter, Sandy Leslie, spent a day there recently, talking to some of those who come face to face with the public in the course of their work at the airport.

Sandy: Well, here I am in one of the airport terminals and it's certainly very busy. I've started at the Information Desk, and I'm talking to Carol Bennett, Information Assistant, while she's having a break from dealing with people's enquiries. Carol, you've certainly got a busy job here, haven't you? There are constant queues, aren't there?

Carol: Yes, they all turn up here at the Information Desk with their problems. If we can't deal with them ourselves, we can refer them to where they need to go, whether it be the medical centre or the chapel or the airline or the shopping mall. The thing about Gatwick Airport is it's like a small town, with all the problems of a small town - lots of people with small problems or large problems, and they all seem to come to this desk.

Sandy: Are there any recent cases that stick out in your mind?

Carol: Well, we had a young lady who came up one day, completely disorientated. She thought she was in Australia. She said 'Am I in Australia?' I said 'No, you're in Gatwick.' She said 'You've got to be joking, I should be in Australia!' I said 'What do you mean?', she said she'd fallen asleep on the aircraft and it was a multi-stop aircraft and of course instead of getting off in Australia, she'd slept right through and got off at Gatwick. I had a lot of trouble getting through to her. She kept trying to show me her ticket, she just couldn't believe what had happened. Of course, she had no luggage, no clothes or anything. It was a terrible shame really – I mean, it might be difficult to imagine how it happened, but it really did, and I wouldn't like it to happen to me. Anyway, I had to contact Travel Care – they handle that sort of thing – and they sorted her out ...

Sandy: Of course, security is a major issue at airports these days and I'm now talking to Richard Willis, Terminal Duty Officer. He's part of the Terminal Duty team, and their job is to keep a constant watch on every corner of the airport, looking out for trouble.

Richard: As you can see, our cameras here in the Monitoring Centre cover the whole of the airport, we can see everything really. The Monitoring Centre is the nerve centre. The information that we get from the cameras is very varied and the staff here will deal with it as best they can and also pass any relevant information on to the members of the Duty Team who are out and about in the building. It can be anything from a medical emergency or a fire alarm anywhere in the building to passenger congestion within the check-in area at very busy times. And basically, with regard to that, the staff will go down there and hopefully sort the problem out so that passengers can have speedy access through the airport to board the aircraft ...

Sandy: I'm now here with Jane Anderson. And Jane, your job involves dealing with sudden problems, doesn't it?

Jane: Yes, I'm in Passenger Services, and I suppose that one of the biggest problems I have, since my job involves both departing and incoming passengers, is, if there are ever any flight delays, these lounges aren't big enough to hold everyone who's kept waiting. There aren't enough seats, so we have people standing and I'm very limited as to how long I can keep them there. The captain's going to be saying to me 'Hold them there for another half an hour' and I'm going 'Well, I can't really do that' and meanwhile obviously they become very agitated because it's so congested in there.

Sandy: All big airports like Gatwick have shopping centres in them and I'm now talking to …

PAUSE 10 SECONDS

Now you will hear Part 2 again.

REPEAT - PAUSE 5 SECONDS

That is the end of Part 2. Now turn to Part 3.

PART 3

You will hear five different radio advertisements for places where parties can be held. For questions 19–23, choose from the list A–F what each place states. Use the letters only once. There is one extra letter which you do not need to use.

You now have 30 seconds in which to look at Part 3.

PAUSE 30 SECONDS

Advertisement 1   Looking for somewhere to hold your party? Look no further than *Marty's*, where both large and small parties are welcome. We'll lay on a feast of nine dishes plus dessert, and vegetarians are catered for. If you want entertainment, we have a lunchtime and evening disco available on selected dates. We can cater for parties of up to 400 and prices start from £16 a head. So contact our Party Office now on 43967740 for further details and bookings.

PAUSE 2 SECONDS

Advertisement 2   If you want to throw that party that people are still talking about months later, come to us at the ever-popular *Hotspot* and we'll organize everything for you. Nightly entertainment includes non-stop live bands, top-class cabaret and the best disco in town. What's more, drinks are half-price on certain days! Larger parties can be accommodated in private suites if you prefer and you can choose from three or four course meals or the special Party Menu, which is £17.50 a head. So call us on 564 3211 for the party with great food, great company and a great atmosphere.

PAUSE 2 SECONDS

Advertisement 3   For the very best in food and service, hold your party at *Bentley's*. We're recommended in all the major restaurant guides, and by newspaper, magazine and radio critics. We'll guarantee the best value in town – you just can't beat our prices! Four and five course menus are available from £14 and there's our excellent buffet menu. We're conveniently right at the heart of the city and we're open every day of the week. So don't delay, contact us now for information and bookings on 94 3521.

PAUSE 2 SECONDS

Advertisement 4   Why not have your party afloat? Let your guests take it easy aboard *The Explorer*, as they cruise along the river. Dancing, with our top-rated DJ, is always available and the food is good. You can hire *The Explorer* for either daytime or evening parties. There's plenty of room for large groups of up to 400 and we've still got a few dates available this month. Prices range from £10 to £13 a head, and you can be sure there are no hidden extras. So for unbeatable value book now on 657 4322.

PAUSE 2 SECONDS

Advertisement 5   For that special occasion, book now at *The Palace*. You'll get a rather sophisticated atmosphere in a lovely location by the river, with great food. We're open seven days a week and we can cater for both lunchtime and evening parties. Parties of 100 or more can take advantage of our delightful Function Room, which comes with no hire charge for the room. Prices start at £10 a head, plus drinks, for our two-course menu, and one or two dates are still available for last-minute bookings. So call us now, on 213 5546.

PAUSE 10 SECONDS

Now you will hear Part 3 again.

REPEAT - PAUSE 5 SECONDS

That is the end of Part 3. Now turn to Part 4.

PART 4

You will hear an interview with someone who started a news service called Children's Express. For questions 24–30, choose the best answer A, B or C.

You now have one minute in which to look at Part 4.

PAUSE ONE MINUTE

Presenter: Welcome back. I'm talking to Bob Wilson, who started *Children's Express*, which is an organization that supplies reports and articles to newspapers, magazines and TV and radio stations in the US. And as we heard before the break, *Children's Express* is entirely staffed by children – they do the interviews, they put together the reports. Bob, is it intended that the children should become journalists?

Bob: Well, although many of them do, it's really about children beginning to look at the world in a different way, beginning to think about the serious issues in the world today. We want them to be responsible citizens when they grow up and in the meantime, they have some powerful messages to deliver to the adult world. And of course, if kids get responsibility for covering the world, it's amazing how interested they become - you know, they begin to read newspapers and news magazines, they think about issues, so it's a really stimulating exercise for them.

Presenter: Now tell me about your youngsters. How old are they and where do they come from?

Bob: They range from eight to eighteen. They're broken down into reporters and editors – the reporters are thirteen and under and they're guided by editors who are fourteen to eighteen years old. All the training is done by the teenage editors, there's no adult involvement at all – the training is passed down from generation to generation. The kids come from the widest possible backgrounds. There are kids from poor economic backgrounds and we'll get some middle-class kids as well, so it's a real mix.

Presenter: And, erm, where have their stories appeared?

Bob: Well, we've done television and we've done radio on the most important radio shows in public radio in the US, and, uh, we've gone into major newspapers and been published in features sections of newspapers which are read by adults. So we're very proud of the adult readership, they're the ones after all that have the vote and the influence.

Presenter: That's quite an achievement isn't it, to have reached a situation where in fact you're taken very seriously by serious newspapers.

Bob: We have a major newspaper that we report for every week, we do a full page for the *Indianapolis Star* every week. They did a readership survey and they found that forty eight per cent of their readers read us either all the time or some of the time and they didn't even measure the child readership, which is very broad. So we were quite excited by that, that we were read - as I understand it - even more than their editorial page.

Presenter: And do you find that, erm, people will cooperate? I mean do they, for example, interview political leaders, do they get access to significant public figures?

Bob: Our kids have interviewed all recent US presidents and many other leaders. So I'd say that the children are taken seriously and they have a background, you know, we've been in business for nineteen years now so that they've been at it for a long time and I think we're quite well-respected in the US media business.

Presenter: Do the children take notes or are the interviews recorded as they're being done?

Bob: Everything is recorded on tape.

Presenter: And do the youngsters rewrite and edit their own stuff under guidance?

Bob: Our kind of journalism for newspapers and magazines – just so you get some idea of why it's so readable by adults – we call it oral journalism. Everything that the children do is tape recorded. The young reporters do the interviews and these are recorded. The teenage editors take notes during the interviews. Then the teenage editors question the reporters about the interviews and this questioning is recorded too. All of that recorded material is then typed out and the young editors then piece the articles together from that. So they don't rewrite, everything is edited from those recordings. Everything in the articles is either the words of the person being interviewed or the words of the child who interviews them. So it's a rather unique form of journalism.

Presenter: You're proud of what you've done, you're proud of your children, aren't you?

Bob: Very proud.

Presenter: Well, we wish you luck.

Bob: It's been a great pleasure, thank you.

Presenter: Right, a short break and then it's sport.

PAUSE 10 SECONDS

Now you will hear Part 4 again.

REPEAT - PAUSE 5 SECONDS

That is the end of Part 4.

There will now be a pause of five minutes for you to copy your answers onto the separate answer sheet. Your supervisor will then collect all the question papers and answer sheets.

TEST 2

First Certificate Listening Test. I am going to give you the instructions for this test. I will introduce each part of the test and give you time to look at the questions. At the start of each piece you will hear this sound.

You will hear each piece twice. Remember, while you are listening, write your answers on the question paper. You will have time at the end of the test to copy your answers onto the separate answer sheet.

The tape will now be stopped. Please ask any questions now, because you must not speak during the test.

PAUSE 5 SECONDS

Now open your question paper and look at Part 1.

PART 1

You will hear people talking in eight different situations. For questions 1–8, choose the best answer A, B or C.

1   You hear someone describing something that happened to her. How did she feel?
  A   annoyed
  B   confused
  C   disappointed

PAUSE 5 SECONDS

Well, I'd been in this country for about a year and I thought I knew the way things were, but I obviously didn't have a grasp on some things. I thought that you were supposed to take a present on occasions like that, but I was the only one who did. I felt pretty bad because I was expecting that everyone else would have done the same, so I didn't really know what was going on – only that I'd got it wrong.

PAUSE 2 SECONDS - REPEAT - PAUSE 2 SECONDS

2   You hear part of a radio play. Where are the speakers?
  A   in a taxi
  B   at an airport
  C   at home

PAUSE 5 SECONDS

Man: I think we're going to miss it. Er... did you lock up and switch everything off?

Woman: Stop worrying. Everything's under control. I checked everything.

Man: Have you got the tickets and the passports?

Woman: Yes, they're in my pocket. Look, we're not going to be late, we've only got a short way to go.

Man: But we're supposed to arrive an hour before the flight.

Woman: I know, but don't worry. It's only round the corner now.

PAUSE 2 SECONDS - REPEAT - PAUSE 2 SECONDS

3   You hear this announcement in a supermarket. What does the announcer want customers to do?
  A   leave the building now
  B   buy a certain product
  C   use a particular exit

PAUSE 5 SECONDS

We would like to inform all customers that our opening hours are from 8am to 7pm every day and that we will shortly be closing. There is still time for you to take advantage of the numerous bargains available in the store, such as the fresh bread, and we hope that you will do so. Please leave through the door behind the checkouts, as the other doors are about to be locked. Thank you.

PAUSE 2 SECONDS - REPEAT - PAUSE 2 SECONDS

4   You hear two people talking on a railway station platform. What is the relationship between them?
  A   They are strangers.
  B   They are colleagues.
  C   They are neighbours.

PAUSE 5 SECONDS

Woman: Do you catch this train very often?

Man: Yes, quite regularly. I have meetings in London about every two weeks.

Woman: Do you find it an easy journey?

Man: It depends. It can take me quite a long time to get here from the area where I live, but sometimes it's not too bad. How about you?

Woman: I live just around the corner so it's no problem for me. I go quite regularly on business as well.

Man: Ah, the train's coming now, right on time.

PAUSE 2 SECONDS - REPEAT - PAUSE 2 SECONDS

5   You hear someone describing a trip. What did she do during the trip?
  A   She spent a lot of money.
  B   She visited a lot of famous places.
  C   She met a lot of people.

PAUSE 5 SECONDS

I had a great time actually. I did all the tourist things and I saw all the sights, but what's wrong with that? I mean, if you go to such a historic city, there's no point in just sitting around in cafés or spending all your time with the other people in the party, is there? There were loads of really good souvenirs in some of the places I went to, but they cost a fortune so I didn't bother with them.

PAUSE 2 SECONDS - REPEAT - PAUSE 2 SECONDS

6   You hear the presenter of a local radio news programme.
    Who is he going to interview?
    A   a member of the public
    B   a local reporter
    C   a senior politician

PAUSE 5 SECONDS

The recent elections have produced some surprising results, so let's find out what's behind this story. Our reporter, Jackie Walsh, has already spoken to the winners and losers and found out their theories, but what about the people who decided the issue? Jackie knows the area better than most and she's been out and about gathering opinions from the people who really count, the voters themselves. So let's find out her conclusions.

PAUSE 2 SECONDS - REPEAT - PAUSE 2 SECONDS

7   You hear someone describing the place where she lives.
    What does she think of the place?
    A   It is dangerous.
    B   It is strange.
    C   It is interesting.

PAUSE 5 SECONDS

I've heard a lot of people saying how risky it is around here, and you hear all these stories about violence and burglaries and all that but, I mean … maybe my experience is totally out of the ordinary, but … I've never come across any of that. For me it's just a place full of the most fantastic mixture of people, I mean, there's always something going on, it's just so full of … of life!

PAUSE 2 SECONDS - REPEAT - PAUSE 2 SECONDS

8   You hear an announcement about a radio programme. What kind of programme is it?
    A   a sports programme
    B   a holiday programme
    C   a health programme

PAUSE 5 SECONDS

Feeling run down? Not getting enough exercise? Need a break? Then you'd better listen to 'Getting away from it all' at 8.30 on Tuesday, where you'll get all sorts of ideas for doing something about it. From a gentle round of golf to a weekend of intensive workouts at a health club, we'll be covering places to suit all pockets. And also, there'll be a special feature on bargain destinations for late bookings. Don't miss it!

PAUSE 2 SECONDS - REPEAT - PAUSE 2 SECONDS

That is the end of Part 1. Now turn to Part 2.

PART 2

You will hear part of a local radio programme, in which the presenter gives details of a competition. For questions 9–18, fill in the missing information.

You now have 45 seconds in which to look at Part 2.

PAUSE 45 SECONDS

OK, finally we come to the competition I mentioned at the start of the programme. It's for any of you out there who fancy yourselves as radio reporters and it's open to anyone, of any age, who is living, working or studying in this area. Perhaps you've listened to this station and thought 'I can do better than that!' Well, this is your chance.

Now, if you want to go in for the competition, what you have to do is to put together and send in a short report on tape, of up to four minutes in length, that deals with something to do with this area. It could be about almost anything, as long as it's connected with this area. You see, what we want you to send in are pieces which

capture the special nature of the area - its people, what goes on here, the things that people care about here, that kind of thing. You might want to go out and interview people, or you could simply describe something, or both - it's up to you.

What about the prizes? Well, the top prize, for the best report overall, is the magnificent Rubicon 2000 portable tape recorder. It's what the professionals use when they're out on a story. It's got a separate microphone for conducting on-the-spot interviews and all the latest in new technology for the professional reporter. In addition, there will be prizes of Candida XR tape recorders for the most interesting subject, the best interview and the most imaginative presentation.

Right, if you want to go in for this competition, here are the details. First of all, the different categories you can enter reports for. Well, there are two main categories. The first is for local personalities and activities. For this, you might choose as your subject someone well-known in your district or a local sports event or festival, for example. The second is for issues of importance in the area today - you might, for example, compile a report about an environmental matter such as traffic problems for this category.

In addition, there's a special category for entries from schools, because we're very keen to get as many of the local schools as possible involved. In this category, we're offering two cash prizes of five hundred pounds each, and the money can be used for the purchase of any equipment needed by the school – it's up to the winners what they choose. Entries for this category are invited not from individuals but from school classes, and teachers may wish them to be related to a special project which could be organized between now and the closing date of July the eighth.

Our expert judges are going to select the six best reports sent in and these will be broadcast on September the sixth, on a special programme on this station - 'Our Society Today'.

Anyone entering the competition should make sure that they submit their reports on good quality tape - remember, they're going to be broadcast. And, very important, make sure that your tape is clearly labelled, with your name and address, which category your report is being entered for and its title.

Entries, clearly marked 'Radio Reporter Competition' on the envelope, should arrive here no later than 4pm on Friday July the eighth. Now, if you want us to send your tape back, you'll have to supply us with a stamped, self-addressed envelope of a suitable size. And if you want to pick it up in person, here at the radio station, which you can do at the end of September, you should mark the envelope 'for collection' and we'll put it on one side to hand over to you when you come in.

So get out there and start your reports - and good luck! I'll be back at the same time next week with another edition of the programme, so until then, goodbye.

PAUSE 10 SECONDS

Now you will hear Part 2 again.

REPEAT - PAUSE 5 SECONDS

That is the end of Part 2. Now turn to Part 3.

PART 3

You will hear five different radio reports. For questions 19–23, choose from the list A–F what each reporter is reporting on. Use the letters only once. There is one extra letter which you do not need to use.

You now have 30 seconds in which to look at Part 3.

PAUSE 30 SECONDS

149

Speaker 1   Well, an enormous crowd has turned out. Although the mood seems to be a good one, it's quite obvious how they feel, and how much ordinary people oppose the whole idea. There are people from all walks of life here, including a lot of workers on their lunch break. At the moment, they're listening to the various speakers. A few minutes ago there was an enormous cheer when they were told that there were about fifty thousand of them. And that figure alone indicates just what public opinion is on this matter.

PAUSE 2 SECONDS

Speaker 2   The crowds came pouring onto the streets immediately afterwards and they're making their reaction to this victory clear in no uncertain terms. Everywhere I look there are lines of people coming along the streets from all directions, arms linked, shouting and singing, and it really is the most incredible scene. People are greeting complete strangers as if they've known them all their lives. There's never been anything like it in the history of this city.

PAUSE 2 SECONDS

Speaker 3   As I sit here, I sense an enormous tension among the crowd, a sense of great anticipation. Normally you'd expect a lot of noise, a lot of singing and chanting, but this is such an important day for all the supporters of both sides, with so much to be won and so much to be lost. There's only a matter of, what, four or five minutes to go before the start, and so, soon, we'll find out who's going to be dancing with joy and who's going to be bitterly disappointed.

PAUSE 2 SECONDS

Speaker 4   Well, it's obviously been very well-supported and it certainly seems to have had an effect. A lot of people have probably decided they might as well stay at home but many more have obviously decided to make their way by other means. There's a lot of traffic on the roads and plenty of people have chosen to walk. The leaders say that everything should be back to normal tomorrow and it's possible that further talks will take place tomorrow. But for the time being, it's chaos for many.

PAUSE 2 SECONDS

Speaker 5   Well, there's certainly a very special atmosphere in the air, for what is a very special occasion. People have been pouring into the stadium from all over and there are queues stretching for miles. Expectations among the fans are high for what will be their first live appearance for years. And it's obvious that, whatever the critics say, these fans remain loyal – I think that, when they finally step onto the stage, they're going to go just wild.

PAUSE 10 SECONDS

Now you will hear Part 3 again.

REPEAT - PAUSE 5 SECONDS

That is the end of Part 3. Now turn to Part 4.

PART 4

You will hear part of a radio phone-in programme in which teenagers give advice on relationships between parents and children. For questions 24–30, write Y (YES) next to those views that are expressed by any of the speakers and N (NO) next to those views that are not expressed.

You now have 45 seconds in which to look at Part 4.

PAUSE 45 SECONDS

Presenter: ... I hope that's been of some use. Moving along, we've got Jane on the line. Good evening Jane ...

Jane: Good evening.

Presenter: Hi. Who would you like to speak to, Jane?

Jane: Well, anybody who might have been through the fourteen to eighteen year old age range, which I'm sure they all have, er, with regard to erm that awful subject of helping in the house. (*laughs all round*) I've got a fourteen ... Oh yeah, I can hear everybody laughing ... I've got a fourteen year old boy and an eighteen year old boy, er ... I have given up with the eighteen year old about his bedroom (*giggles*). I decided that he needed his space and if he wished to live in a rubbish tip then so be it, so I've simply closed the door on it. But it is the fact that I work, well, practically full-time, erm, and I could do with a bit of help around the house. But the usual response when I ask them is, er, well either they're doing something else or, whichever son it is erm ... erm, or you know, it's a case of 'Why can't he do it?', meaning his brother. Or if they do actually get round to doing it then it's not very well done – if it's washing up they have water all over the floor. Erm, any tips?

Presenter: Nick, have you got something to say about this?

Nick: Well this sounds like more or less the same relationship that I had with my mum until she discussed it with me. I'm sixteen and if my mother, erm, if she needs help around the house, we have a sort of agreement that, uh, I clean up behind myself, I do any other jobs which look like they should be done, and I often repair things around the house and things like that. So if you maybe tell your children that this is what you want them to do, that they should at the very minimum clean up behind themselves and then do any other jobs that they feel they should do. That sounds to me like a fair agreement and if you try that it might work.

Presenter: Amelia?

Amelia: Well the fact is your children really aren't children any more and you shouldn't really let them get away with it. They're old enough, you know, to realize - and it's not fair, you know, you're their mother and they really should be doing what ... I mean, they live under your roof. I think that all parents have a standard set of rules and that should be one of the rules, that they should do their share around the house. I think your view on, you know, letting your son leave his room, you know, a mess is a very satisfactory one and one that all parents should adopt but really, you know, you're treating them like children if you don't really insist that they help you in the house. Because your sons, especially your older son, they're going to be leaving soon, to be leaving home to go to university or something, and they're not going to have mummy there to do the washing up. They should start learning now, that, you know, chores should be shared in a family.

Presenter: Well Jane, it seems that the answer to all this is that you're letting them off the hook. You tell them – they can't get away with it any longer! (*laughter all round*) Anyway, we're moving on now. If you want to speak to this panel tonight the number is 01325 580 4444, if you want to speak to our panel about any subject to do with parent - children relationships.

PAUSE 10 SECONDS

Now you will hear Part 4 again.

REPEAT - PAUSE 5 SECONDS

That is the end of Part 4.

There will now be a pause of five minutes for you to copy your answers onto the separate answer sheet. Your supervisor will then collect all the question papers and answer sheets.

TEST 3

First Certificate Listening Test. I am going to give you the instructions for this test. I will introduce each part of the test and give you time to look at the questions. At the start of each piece you will hear this sound.

You will hear each piece twice. Remember, while you are listening, write your answers on the question paper. You will have time at the end of the test to copy your answers onto the separate answer sheet.

The tape will now be stopped. Please ask any questions now, because you must not speak during the test.

PAUSE 5 SECONDS

Now open your question paper and look at Part 1.

PART 1

You will hear people talking in eight different situations.

For questions 1–8, choose the best answer A, B or C.

1   You hear a critic describing a film. What is his opinion of it?
    A   It is dull.
    B   It will shock.
    C   It is peculiar.

PAUSE 5 SECONDS

… it seems to me extraordinary that such a film should ever have been made. There's nothing wrong with the cast – they're all excellent actors – but I simply can't imagine that the public are going to like it. It's very violent but the violence is so badly done that it makes you want to laugh. It's not exactly what you'd call original, and I suspect that most people unfortunate enough to go and see it will simply yawn and wait for it to end.

PAUSE 2 SECONDS - REPEAT - PAUSE 2 SECONDS

2   You hear someone talking on a radio phone-in programme. Where is he phoning from?
    A   his home
    B   his car
    C   his place of work

PAUSE 5 SECONDS

… yes, when I heard your last caller I was so annoyed that I … I just had to pull over and call in. Look, it's all very well to sit back and criticize from the comfort of your own home, but if you had a job as hard as that, I mean if you had to go in every day and deal with the sort of things they have to deal with, day in, day out, you'd realize just how hard it is. Anyway, that's all I wanted to say. I'll be on my way now …

PAUSE 2 SECONDS - REPEAT - PAUSE 2 SECONDS

3   You hear part of a radio play. What is the relationship between the speakers?
    A   They went to the same school.
    B   They have met once before.
    C   They are married to each other.

PAUSE 5 SECONDS

Woman: I saw Jack the other day. You know, we haven't seen him since that wedding.

Man: Yeah, what a day that was!

Woman: Yeah. You know, that was the last time our whole class was together.

Man: You're right. Hey, maybe we should try to have another get-together while you're over here.

Woman: That'd be great. Do you think we've got time to organize it before I go back? I haven't seen anyone from the old days since I went away.

Man: I don't know. We could try.

PAUSE 2 SECONDS - REPEAT - PAUSE 2 SECONDS

4   You hear an advertisement on the radio. What is being advertised?
    A   a special offer
    B   new products
    C   a new shop

PAUSE 5 SECONDS

Hurry on down to Topmart. As well as our usual sensational prices, we've got something completely new for you! Our brand new range of the very latest television and video equipment beats anything you'll find anywhere else in town. For visual and audio quality at affordable prices, there's never been anything like it. So come along to Topmart, everyone's favourite store.

PAUSE 2 SECONDS - REPEAT - PAUSE 2 SECONDS

5   You are in an airport when somebody comes and speaks to you. What does he want you to do?
    A   show him where Gate 12 is
    B   get some information for him
    C   explain what he should do

PAUSE 5 SECONDS

Excuse me, did you catch that announcement just then? I heard something about a flight to Madrid – that's where I'm going – but I didn't get what was said exactly. There was something about boarding at Gate 12, I think – Gate 12's over there, according to that sign but I'm not sure whether we're supposed to go through now or wait here for another call. Did you catch it, by any chance?

PAUSE 2 SECONDS - REPEAT - PAUSE 2 SECONDS

6   You hear someone being interviewed on the radio. Who is the speaker?
    A   a composer
    B   an actor
    C   a film director

PAUSE 5 SECONDS

Well, I've always found that it's the director's role that's the really crucial one. He's the one who decides what sort of atmosphere the music's supposed to create and I just take it from there and try to match the sounds to that. Of course, it's the actors that get all the attention – that's only natural – but if I've done my job well, I think that what I do plays just as important a part in whether a film works or not.

PAUSE 2 SECONDS - REPEAT - PAUSE 2 SECONDS

7   You hear someone talking on the telephone. What is she doing?
    A   expressing regret
    B   defending herself
    C   offering to do something

PAUSE 5 SECONDS

I don't know what came over me – it's most unlike me to talk like that, as you know … Look, I can perfectly well see your point of view and I've got no excuse. I wish I'd never opened my big mouth … Yes, I appreciate how upsetting it was, but all I can say is, it won't happen again, I promise you. I mean, if it's any comfort to you, I feel just as bad about it as you do.

PAUSE 2 SECONDS - REPEAT - PAUSE 2 SECONDS

8   You hear the presenters of a radio programme talking. What are they going to do?
    A   find out about a city
    B   compare different cities
    C   visit a market

PAUSE 5 SECONDS

Woman: Well, here we are right in the heart of the city and it's certainly full of noise and activity, isn't it Harry?

Man: Yes, in fact we're talking to you from one of the many colourful markets that you can find all over the city, and I don't think I've seen such a variety of food for sale anywhere else in the world.

Woman: It really is something, isn't it. Well, for the next half hour, join us as we have a good look round various districts here and talk to the locals in our search for the real New York. Is there really nowhere else like it?

PAUSE 2 SECONDS - REPEAT - PAUSE 2 SECONDS

That is the end of Part 1. Now turn to Part 2.

PART 2

You will hear part of a travel programme, in which a reporter talks about various ferries. For questions 9–18, fill in the missing information.

You now have 45 seconds in which to look at Part 2.

PAUSE 45 SECONDS

Presenter: OK, now we come to our regular review spot, and this week we look at ferries. Every year hundreds of thousands of people take them across the sea from Britain to other parts of Europe, and we sent our reporter Alice Little to find out what they're really like. Alice, the first one you took was the *Sea Master* – what did you make of it?

Alice: Yes, well I was particularly impressed by how friendly and competent the staff were, and overall this boat gave me a good trip. It has one bar and four restaurants – there's nothing special about those, but they're adequate – and a children's area. The main problem for me was in the shops – they were much too crowded to make shopping easy and I could have done without being packed in there like a sardine.

Presenter: Marks out of ten?

Alice: I'd say about seven.

Presenter: Which boat was next?

Alice: Well, then I went on the *Maid of the Ocean*. This one has a very large bar full of video machines – if you like that sort of thing – one main restaurant and a smaller self-service snack bar. I thought the children's area stood out here – there were lots of games laid on and there was a kids' video room there, which is a really good idea. On the downside, I felt that there just weren't enough signs – I couldn't find my way around and I kept getting lost when I went to get my car. So, I'd give this one six out of ten.

Presenter: OK, next we sent you on the *Europa*. What did you make of that?

Alice: On the whole I enjoyed this trip, especially because of the comfortable seating. There was plenty of room in the seats and there were train-style compartments for up to six passengers, which are ideal if you want to play games. There are two big bars and one cafeteria – they weren't bad – and a simple kids' area. Unfortunately, a minus on this boat was that it was rather dirty – it didn't look as if it had been cleaned up since the last trip.

Presenter: Marks out of ten?

Alice: I think seven.

Presenter: Did any boat score more than seven?

Alice: Yes, one. I'd give eight or nine to the *Sea Breeze* – I thought it was the best of the lot. It's a brand-new boat – I think it's only been in service for a couple of weeks – and I really enjoyed my trip on it. For me the biggest plus point was the range of food – in the four restaurants you could get everything from a quick snack and fast food to a superb four-course meal, that would not disgrace a very good city restaurant. If I have a criticism, it's that it's got this horrible design – there are too many patterns everywhere and it looks more like a floating shopping centre than a boat.

Presenter: OK, so that was the best. Which one was the worst?

Alice: Well I couldn't give more than five out of ten to the *Western Pride*, I'm afraid. It wasn't really to do with the boat itself – it had one or two things to recommend it, particularly the bargains in the shops – I picked up a few things there at low prices, so I certainly had no complaints on that subject. No, the big problem was the queues. Everywhere you went, everything you wanted to do, there were always endless queues. It drove me mad and really spoiled the trip.

Presenter: And finally?

Alice: Yes, finally, I went on the *Blue Lagoon* and I suppose this was about average, say six out of ten. One really good thing this one has is the 'fun room', which has video games, fruit machines and all manner of hi-tech amusements – it was certainly very popular with families. In the brochure they talk a lot about the restaurants and snack bars on this boat, but I have to report that the poor quality of the food in them really put me off. Everything I had was either overcooked or undercooked and I had a burger that was so disgusting I couldn't finish it. Not exactly what you want on a sea crossing!

Presenter: Well, on that note, thanks for your views, Alice. Next week Alice will be comparing flights on different airlines …

PAUSE 10 SECONDS

Now you will hear Part 2 again.

REPEAT - PAUSE 5 SECONDS

That is the end of Part 2. Now turn to Part 3.

PART 3

You will hear five different people talking about a famous entertainer. For questions 19–23, choose which of the opinions A–F each speaker expresses. Use the letters only once. There is one extra letter which you do not need to use.

You now have 30 seconds in which to look at Part 3.

PAUSE 30 SECONDS

Speaker 1   I think that behind that image, everything isn't quite what it seems. You know, all that stuff in the papers about his private life – well, he hasn't exactly been lucky there, has he? I mean, you can have all the talent in the world, and all the fame, but what use is that if your life's a mess? He might *look* easy-going and all that, but I reckon he's actually suffering a lot of the time.

PAUSE 2 SECONDS

Speaker 2   It seems to me that you can't switch on the TV or open a magazine without seeing his face. It's typical, though, these days, isn't it? I mean, it's just ridiculous – people like him, they come out of nowhere, suddenly everyone's talking about them and then it's here today, gone tomorrow. It's got nothing to do with whether you're any good or not, has it? It's the media – they focus all that attention on them and then they just drop them.

PAUSE 2 SECONDS

Speaker 3   I know everyone says how fantastic he is and all that, but personally I just can't see it. I mean, there are plenty of people around who could do what he does – I don't think it takes anything special. I think all those things people say about how great he is, well it's so stupid, he doesn't deserve it at all. Mind you, there are people like him who seem to manage to stay at the top for ages, even though in all honesty they haven't got much to offer.

PAUSE 2 SECONDS

Speaker 4   Well, he may or may not be any good at what he does – I'm not really in a position to know about that – but frankly you can't expect to carry on like that in public and be taken seriously. I mean, I'd be far too embarrassed, but he obviously doesn't care or he wouldn't act like that, would he? Really, though, it's not exactly amusing, what he does, is it? I don't think he ought to be allowed to get away with it – someone ought to tell him to be quiet, very soon.

PAUSE 2 SECONDS

Speaker 5   I wouldn't let that smile fool you – I mean, he's no idiot, he knows exactly what he's doing, he's got his image all worked out. It's obvious he wants to stay at the top for as long as he can. He's got it all planned. That 'everybody's friend' act he puts on, he's obviously just pretending. He must hope nobody notices, and I suppose most people don't. Underneath it, though, he's incredibly ambitious, I reckon.

PAUSE 10 SECONDS

Now you will hear Part 3 again.

REPEAT - PAUSE 5 SECONDS

That is the end of Part 3. Now turn to Part 4.

PART 4

You will hear part of an interview with a man who has spent some time living on a desert island. For questions 24–30, choose the best answer A, B or C.

You now have one minute in which to look at Part 4.

PAUSE 1 MINUTE

Interviewer: Tony Williams' book, *Island of Dreams*, is less like a travel book than most I've read. It's the true story of one man's, one family's, search for paradise. It's an amazing book, but it's a book full of disappointment for a man in search of a bit of perfection. You're a dreamer, aren't you, Tony? At the beginning of the book you're fairly innocent and fairly naive.

Tony: Yes, I've always had dreams since my younger days, when I was absorbed in so many books – my dreams have always come from books. And when I first went to the island it was my first voyage out of Britain and I was shocked by the beauty, by the colour. It was a strange and wonderful experience.

Interviewer: So you went there - what were you looking for?

Tony: I was looking for total escape, release from stress. While I was in Britain I'd been working so many years and getting into increasing debt with electricity, gas and there were so many bills and I had a young family and I thought I needed … I'd been reading about a man called Tom Nealy in the 1950s, he lived on a desert island for several years and I was just looking to get away from society, so I decided to do that.

Interviewer: It didn't work though. You had to go back to Britain.

Tony: Yes, I got to this uninhabited island with my wife Kathy. I had no sort of financial backing and I could only afford a cheap tent … and it was very small and I had this knife and this fishing net. I was unprepared and it was very difficult on our island. Er … we couldn't climb the coconut trees to get coconuts to eat, and I'm unable to swim so we found some difficulty in fishing. If we'd had anybody to collect us, we would have left the island after a few days. Because we were left there without any of the local divers coming to collect us, we adjusted and we managed after the first few months.

Presenter: But you left.

Tony: We left the island first of all because we'd left the children with Kathy's parents so that we could see whether we could survive on the island. We went back to Britain – I only had six months' leave of absence, without pay, from my employers. Then when we went back to Britain, I had this accident and I lost my job and I wanted to go back to the island with my children, with the family as a whole.

Interviewer: So you went back to the island … and at this stage … you give details in the book about the sunburn, the fishing and all the rest of it that you had to do, and there's a wonderful description of a storm.

Tony: Yes, after the first week or so on the island for the second time, we had a hurricane. The calm lagoon turned into huge waves, our tent nearly blew away and there was fear but we didn't want to show it to our children because they looked up to us. I thought I needed to tie my four-year-old daughter to a palm tree for safety but it didn't happen because she was a bit scared. There was a lot of noise on the island, there were a lot of frigate-birds and mynah birds and a few hours prior to the storm everything went quiet as if the animals sensed what was coming, but we didn't realize that at the time. The storm lasted one night and half a day and the island was in a bit of a mess after that.

Interviewer: You're back in Britain now to promote the book, but are you going back to the island?

Tony: I came back to Britain with my family but I'm homesick for the island.

Interviewer: What about your wife?

Tony: She's had a taste of the South Seas and she wants to go back there.

Interviewer: If you went back, would you find it easy to survive?

Tony: Well, what I found on our island, which was strange – all the years I was working, for ten years I was working twelve-hour shifts and I wasn't progressing, there wasn't any money, still a search for money to find to pay our bills. But on our island we had the coconuts for food, fish, crabs, rice, there were wild chickens, and we found we could survive on the island with the food that was there. Still, we would take more supplies with us next time.

Interviewer: Would you take the kids with you next time, and would you go forever?

Tony: This is what we've discussed and what we've decided is when we get back as a family to the island, if for any reason the children say, 'We've been here for a few months, we want to go back home, it's not for us', then I would return with them until they became independent and that's when I would go back to the island for good.

Interviewer: Well, it's a wonderful story and if you read it, it tells you a lot about yourself and your own reactions. Tony Williams, thanks for coming.

Tony: Thank you.

PAUSE 10 SECONDS

Now you will hear Part 4 again.

REPEAT - PAUSE 5 SECONDS

That is the end of Part 4.

There will now be a pause of five minutes for you to copy your answers onto the separate answer sheet. Your supervisor will then collect all the question papers and answer sheets.

TEST 4

First Certificate Listening Test. I am going to give you the instructions for this test. I will introduce each part of the test and give you time to look at the questions. At the start of each piece you will hear this sound.

You will hear each piece twice. Remember, while you are listening, write your answers on the question paper. You will have time at the end of the test to copy your answers onto the separate answer sheet.

The tape will now be stopped. Please ask any questions now, because you must not speak during the test.

PAUSE 5 SECONDS

Now open your question paper and look at Part 1.

PART 1

You will hear people talking in eight different situations. For questions 1–8, choose the best answer A, B or C.

1   *You hear a critic on the radio talking about a book. What is his main criticism of the book?*
    A   The style is poor.
    B   The plot is too complicated.
    C   The characters are not believable.

PAUSE 5 SECONDS

Well, this was one I couldn't really get into at all. Of course, everyone talks about his highly individual style and I wouldn't dispute that. He's certainly a very imaginative writer and some of the characters in this one get up to some pretty astonishing things, but I felt that it was all a bit too clever for its own good. There are all sorts of characters who come in and then disappear – in the end I just couldn't follow what was going on, so I gave up.

PAUSE 2 SECONDS - REPEAT - PAUSE 2 SECONDS

2   *You hear someone talking about a time when she was a student abroad. What did she particularly like?*
    A   the school she studied at
    B   the town she stayed in
    C   the family she stayed with

PAUSE 5 SECONDS

Yeah, I really enjoyed it, I couldn't have gone to a better place. The family did their best ... to be honest I wasn't all that keen on them, though – they were talking to me all the time, they just wouldn't leave me alone. The teachers were nice enough ... mind you, I don't think I learnt anything I couldn't have got out of reading a book at home. Still, none of that bothered me because there was just so much to do there. I was out every night, at all sorts of different places, and I met some great people!

PAUSE 2 SECONDS - REPEAT - PAUSE 2 SECONDS

3   *You hear a radio interviewer introducing a guest. Who is the guest?*
    A   a scientist
    B   a businessman
    C   an inventor

PAUSE 5 SECONDS

My next guest is a man who started with nothing and now has the world at his feet. From humble origins in a poor family, he is now responsible for equipment found in homes throughout the country. He spotted the possibilities of the new computer technology twenty years ago and he made it affordable to people in general. While others were afraid to take the risk, he jumped in and set up the operation that now has the largest slice of the personal computer market. Ladies and gentlemen, Derek Woodrow.

PAUSE 2 SECONDS - REPEAT - PAUSE 2 SECONDS

4   *You hear a caller on a radio phone-in programme. What feeling does the caller express?*
    A   sympathy
    B   self-pity
    C   envy

PAUSE 5 SECONDS

I think the previous caller ought to thank her lucky stars! I mean, she's got a choice of three jobs and she doesn't know which one to take! If only I was in her position ... I've been applying for months and nobody's offered me anything, but you won't find me complaining. I mean, she might think she's got a problem, but I wouldn't mind having a problem like that.

PAUSE 2 SECONDS - REPEAT - PAUSE 2 SECONDS

5   *You hear part of a radio interview. Who is being interviewed?*
    A   a customer at a shop
    B   the manager of a shop
    C   someone who lives near a shop

PAUSE 5 SECONDS

Interviewer: So how do you feel about criticisms of the new store?

Man: Well, I can understand them, especially from people who live nearby and are worried about all the traffic that'll come here. But it's going to be so convenient. People from all over the area will be able to shop at leisure and park easily and I can guarantee that the service will be excellent. It only opened two days ago and already shoppers are flocking here. After all, value for money is what they all want.

PAUSE 2 SECONDS - REPEAT - PAUSE 2 SECONDS

6   *You hear someone talking on a public telephone. What does she want the other person to do?*
    A   explain something he said
    B   apologize to someone
    C   give an honest opinion

PAUSE 5 SECONDS

Why don't you just accept that you were in the wrong, tell her you accept that, and that'll be the end of it. I mean, you're just so stubborn, aren't you, you just can't see that you're not always right. Come on, why not change the habits of a lifetime for once and tell her that you shouldn't have said what you said? It's not that difficult you know, and it'll really do some good.

PAUSE 2 SECONDS - REPEAT - PAUSE 2 SECONDS

7   *You hear someone talking at the Information Desk in an airport. What is his situation?*
   A   He has missed his flight.
   B   He has come to meet someone.
   C   He thinks there is a message for him.

PAUSE 5 SECONDS

Man: Has the flight from Zurich arrived yet?

Assistant: Yes, about half an hour ago.

Man: The one that stops here and then goes on to Hong Kong?

Assistant: Yes.

Man: Oh dear, I've been waiting in the wrong place. Have all the passengers been through yet?

Assistant: I should think so.

Man: Oh no, they've probably given up and gone. Is there any way you could put out a message in case they're still here?

PAUSE 2 SECONDS - REPEAT - PAUSE 2 SECONDS

8   *You hear the presenter talking at the beginning of a radio programme. What is the programme going to be about?*
   A   how to eat healthily
   B   new food products
   C   eating habits

PAUSE 5 SECONDS

Welcome to the programme. In this series we've looked at the latest goods on the market in the world of food, and we've looked in depth at what to eat if you want to stay fit and well. Today we look at how much the advertising of new products influences what we eat, and how much attention people pay to advice about healthy eating. I can promise you there are some surprising statistics coming up ...

PAUSE 2 SECONDS - REPEAT - PAUSE 2 SECONDS

That is the end of Part 1. Now turn to Part 2.

PART 2

You will hear a talk given to a class by a young woman, in which she talks about her career so far as an actress and director. For questions 9–18, fill in the missing information.

You now have 45 seconds in which to look at Part 2.

PAUSE 45 SECONDS

What made me want to be a performer? Perhaps it's in the blood – I'm the great grand-daughter of an opera singer. I set my sights on the stage at an early age. Ballet was my first love but I grew too tall and so my ambition switched to acting. I took part in as many school productions as I could and I ended up studying Theatre Studies at university. Four years ago, I left university, having secured a place on an acting course at a drama school in London.

The course was just for one year, a year which I had to finance myself. I hadn't lived in London before – I come from a small seaside town – so it was quite a culture shock. Having to find the money was a strain – it was quite an expensive course – and I also had great difficulty finding somewhere to live that I could afford in London. Eventually, I managed to rent a flat with a couple of other students on the course. I found the first few weeks of the course really stressful and tiring but a few weeks on, I really got into it. It boosted my confidence and it was much more on the practical side – we only had to do one theory thing.

When the course ended I was one of 565 students to graduate from a recognized drama course that summer. I was fortunate enough to get a job straight away with a theatre company outside London, working in Drama in Education. We went to lots of schools and I really enjoyed it. After that I went back to London and it was really hard, because it was the first time in my life I had nothing to do. I'd always written essays or learnt lines and performed and now I was unemployed. I wrote lots of letters looking for work – Wednesdays and Thursdays were my main letter-writing days. I went to see plays as much as I could, so that I could then write to the Artistic Managers and say 'I saw your production, would it be possible to come and meet you' - then I met him or her and I was at least on file – that way they might remember me if a part came up that was suitable for me. It's estimated that actors spend as much as eighty per cent of their time looking for work. Someone told me that for every twenty letters you write you may get an audition and for every twenty auditions you may get a job.

Then my long-awaited break came. I got a job in a production called *A Christmas Carol* in a small theatre. It was a profit-sharing arrangement – this means you only get paid if the play makes a profit. Not many people came – we thought we'd done well if we got twenty people in the audience, and one night there were only six. So it didn't do anything to make my financial situation any better. But it's amazing how much better you feel when you actually get a part – it made a huge difference to how I felt about myself.

I then began to turn my attention from acting to directing, in an attempt to take more control of my situation. I directed *The Illusion* at the Dukes Head Theatre and it got good reviews, but it was another profit-share arrangement and I still had money problems. I kept thinking that I would be successful and something was going to change. You've got to make your own luck, so each day I did something towards the plan of success. I made a couple of important phone calls each day, asking large theatre companies to come and see the play I was directing.

I then set up my own company, the King's Players, and directed a production of *A Family Affair*, which won the London Small Theatre award for Best Comedy Production. We had a couple of lovely photos in national newspapers and some great reviews and that was great because I could now be taken seriously as a director. Then I decided to try to appear in a TV commercial for coffee – I read that they were looking for somebody, so I wrote off, I thought 'you never know' and I got a phone call from the company saying that I had been shortlisted right down from five thousand to the last eleven. But I didn't get it, which was a shame because I was fed up with working for no money. The one good thing that came out of it, though, was that I got an agent, one of the two main agents that cast all the adverts, so I'm waiting to hear about others.

I now want to get a position as an assistant director with a major company, I think that's the next step, not just for the money. I think I'm at my best when directing, I mean it's horrible on the first night when it's beyond your control, you can't do anything if something goes wrong, and it is quite lonely. But I am very happy and I have greater satisfaction when things work than with acting, so I think this is the way I'm going to go.

Four years ago when I started I thought I'd be further on than I am now – I didn't envisage being unemployed for such long periods. I feel that I've developed and matured – before, I presumed that I would be successful. Now, I still know that I will be successful ultimately, but it may not be simple – it may take longer and be much harder than I anticipated. That's what I've learnt. Nothing depresses me more than the idea of getting old and thinking that I never really tried and I never made it because I gave up.

PAUSE 10 SECONDS

Now you will hear Part 2 again.

REPEAT - PAUSE 5 SECONDS

That is the end of Part 2. Now turn to Part 3.

PART 3

You will hear five different people talking about a concert on a radio phone-in programme. For questions 19–23, choose from the list A–F what each speaker is doing. Use the letters only once. There is one extra letter which you do not need to use.

You now have 30 seconds in which to look at Part 3.

PAUSE 30 SECONDS

Speaker 1   Yeah, well Barry, I went along the other night and what I want to know is, why did they only play for 40 minutes? I mean, we paid enough for it, and the programme said they'd be on for an hour and a half. I wouldn't have bothered going if I'd known that was all we were going to get – I mean, it's not exactly fair to the fans is it?

PAUSE 2 SECONDS

Speaker 2   Yes, hello Barry. I heard some of your earlier callers saying how they couldn't see anything, you know, they were too far away and all they could see was the video screens, they couldn't see the band on stage. Well, all I can say is they must have got there too late. We queued up for ages before the doors opened and we got right to the front, really close to the stage. Really, that's what you have to do if you want a good view, even if it does mean a long wait.

PAUSE 2 SECONDS

Speaker 3   It's all right for all these other callers, talking about the concert, but what I want to know is, how do you get in? I mean, I tried everything to get a ticket – I phoned, I wrote, I went to agencies but everywhere I tried, they'd sold out. I must have been going to the wrong places. So, has anyone out there got any ideas where I might have more luck next time?

PAUSE 2 SECONDS

Speaker 4   Barry, you read all that stuff in the press about how they're not as good as they used to be, but you could have fooled me. I just wanted to phone up and say I haven't seen anything like it, and I've been to plenty of their concerts. I read somewhere that they didn't put as much energy into their performance as they used to but all I can say is, whoever wrote that can't have been at the same concert I was at.

PAUSE 2 SECONDS

Speaker 5   Am I the only one who noticed? Surely not. None of your callers so far has said anything about their new look. Personally, I thought it was a bit of a mistake, but what do the other fans make of it? I'd like to know what the general view is. I mean, the new hairstyles and clothes are quite a radical change – do people out there think it's a good move?

PAUSE 10 SECONDS

Now you will hear Part 3 again.

REPEAT - PAUSE 5 SECONDS

That is the end of Part 3. Now turn to Part 4.

PART 4

You will hear an interview with two young people who spent some time travelling abroad. For questions 24–30, write D next to what Dan says, A next to what Anna says and N next to what neither of them says.

You now have 45 seconds in which to look at Part 4.

PAUSE 45 SECONDS

Presenter: These days a lot of young people go 'backpacking' – travelling around with all their possessions in the bag they carry on their back. I have with me today Dan Roberts and Anna Renton, who are going to share some of their experiences of doing just that. Dan, if I can turn to you first, you went round Europe, didn't you?

Dan: Yes, for three weeks in August. I left home at three o'clock on the morning of the first day of the holiday and travelled for 27 hours before arriving at Marseille, the first stop on our itinerary. It was exhausting. After this experience I quickly got used to sleeping in very uncomfortable places – this is the only way to survive such intensive travelling.

Presenter: Now Anna, you spent seven and a half months travelling by yourself in India, Indonesia, Australia and North and South America. That must have been quite an adventure.

Anna: Yes, apart from the occasional family holiday I'd never travelled before I set out on this trip and I was very apprehensive about going on such an ambitious journey. What worried me most was the prospect of being lonely, and the dangers of travelling as a single woman. But in fact I was lonely only occasionally – it was worst at the beginning. After that I was never alone for long stretches because I made a real effort to meet people – if I wanted company I travelled with them.

Presenter: Did you go on your own, Dan?

Dan: No, I travelled with four other people, which was almost too many, but we avoided a lot of potential arguments by carefully planning our route before we left.

Presenter: Did you have any problems with other people, Anna?

Anna: Well, the constant stream of slightly rude comments in some countries made me angry and I felt myself becoming more aggressive in response. Ultimately, these irritations were just something I had to put up with.

Presenter: What about the places you visited?

Dan: Sometimes we had to be flexible about our plans. We found that places described as 'unspoilt and tourist-free' in the guide book can turn out to be obscure villages with nothing to see or do and nowhere for visitors to stay.

Anna: I went with an open mind, really. Some of the places I found myself in were pretty horrible, but that's all part of the experience isn't it?

Presenter: What about places to stay?

Dan: We usually slept in campsites or arranged our journeys so that we could spend the night on the train – that was cheap and relatively comfortable. Youth hostels were all packed in August and much more expensive, so we kept away from them.

Anna: I ended up in some pretty rough places, the sort of places I wouldn't even consider staying in at home, but I didn't mind that because it was all part of the adventure.

Presenter: Did you feel you had to be careful?

Dan: Yes, I'd spoken to people who had lost everything – students on trains seem to be easy targets. So, wherever we were, I always slept with my money and passport at the bottom of my sleeping bag.

Anna: Well, being a woman alone was something I was conscious of throughout the trip. I never felt physically threatened, though I made sure I didn't get into obviously dangerous situations.

Presenter: Did your trip live up to your expectations?

Dan: Well, our tickets were valid for a month but we ran out of money and energy before they expired and came back. We'd seen a huge amount by then but we couldn't keep up our enthusiasm any longer.

Anna: Travelling on such a large scale is very time-consuming and seven and a half months wasn't long enough. If I were to do it again, I don't think I'd try to take on so much.

Presenter: Would you go on similar trips again?

Dan: Yes, I think so – I certainly enjoyed the independence of it all, even though I sometimes had to do things because one of the others wanted to.

Anna: Actually I have travelled by myself again since this trip and will do again. There's an element of selfishness in wanting to travel alone, but you are so much freer when you are able to make your own decisions.

Presenter: Well, thanks to both of you ...

PAUSE 10 SECONDS

Now you will hear Part 4 again.

REPEAT - PAUSE 5 SECONDS

That is the end of Part 4.

There will now be a pause of five minutes for you to copy your answers onto the separate answer sheet. Your supervisor will then collect all the question papers and answer sheets.

TEST 5

First Certificate Listening Test. I am going to give you the instructions for this test. I will introduce each part of the test and give you time to look at the questions. At the start of each piece you will hear this sound.

You will hear each piece twice. Remember, while you are listening, write your answers on the question paper. You will have time at the end of the test to copy your answers onto the separate answer sheet.

The tape will now be stopped. Please ask any questions now, because you must not speak during the test.

PAUSE 5 SECONDS

Now open your question paper and look at Part 1.

PART 1

You will hear people talking in eight different situations. For questions 1–8, choose the best answer A, B or C.

1   *You hear two people talking in a hotel. What is the relationship between them?*
     A   *They are both staying at the hotel.*
     B   *They are both attending the same conference.*
     C   *They are both in the same party of tourists.*

PAUSE 5 SECONDS

Woman: So what do you think of this place then?

Man: Well, it's better than the one I'm in. I'm in some dreadful place round the corner.

Woman: Are you? I thought we were all supposed to be here.

Man: We were, but there was a last-minute change of plan. The meetings are all going to be here though.

Woman: We're in the same group tomorrow, aren't we?

Man: Yes, it's Travel in the Future or something, isn't it?

PAUSE 2 SECONDS - REPEAT - PAUSE 2 SECONDS

2   *You hear someone talking on the telephone. What is she doing?*
     A   *demanding an apology*
     B   *insisting on an action*
     C   *asking for a favour*

PAUSE 5 SECONDS

Look, I'm afraid that simply won't do. You were supposed to be here at three to do these repairs and it's half past four now. I'm not interested in your excuses ... no, you're not sorry at all ... no I'm not being unreasonable ... is it asking too much for you to keep an appointment? ... look, I need it doing now, it won't wait ... no, tomorrow afternoon won't do ...

PAUSE 2 SECONDS - REPEAT - PAUSE 2 SECONDS

3   *You hear an advertisement for a magazine. What does this month's issue have that's unusual?*
     A   *an extra part*
     B   *a special interview*
     C   *a competition*

PAUSE 5 SECONDS

Get this month's issue of *Sports World*. It's better than ever! There are all the usual features, our ever-popular Competition of the Month – this time the prize is two tickets to a major sports event of your choice. Our Star Interview this month is with Gary White. And since the new year is coming up, this month's issue includes a pull-out section containing all the year's major sporting fixtures – a fantastic reference, which you can keep and consult all year. So buy *Sports World*, available at all newsagents, today!

PAUSE 2 SECONDS - REPEAT - PAUSE 2 SECONDS

4   *You hear someone talking about a job interview. How does she feel?*
     A   *She is looking forward to the interview.*
     B   *She is confident of being offered the job.*
     C   *She is not very interested in the job.*

PAUSE 5 SECONDS

Yes, it's tomorrow at 11. I haven't given much thought to it, to tell you the truth. I'm normally pretty nervous before them, but this time I'm not, for some reason. I haven't got a clue what my chances are but that doesn't bother me. It'll just be good to have the opportunity to show what I know – I shouldn't think there'll be all that many questions I can't answer. I'll just go in there and give it my best – I've got nothing to lose.

PAUSE 2 SECONDS - REPEAT - PAUSE 2 SECONDS

5   *You hear someone talking on the telephone. Why won't he go to the party?*
     A   *He feels ill.*
     B   *He has to do something else.*
     C   *He doesn't want to go.*

PAUSE 5 SECONDS

Hello, Suzie, it's Alan ... look, I feel awful about this but I can't come to your party tonight ... something's come up ... no, I can't get out of it, it's a problem I've got to sort out straight away ... I won't go into it now ... yes I know I did this the last time you invited me but don't take it personally ... no, that's not true, I *do* like your friends ... honestly, there's nothing I can do about it ...

PAUSE 2 SECONDS - REPEAT - PAUSE 2 SECONDS

6   *You hear two people talking in a café. What is their opinion of their trip?*
     A   *It cost too much.*
     B   *It is badly organized.*
     C   *The places they visit are boring.*

PAUSE 5 SECONDS

Man: What do you make of it so far then?

Woman: Well, I'm very disappointed. Nobody seems to know what's going on.

Man: I quite agree. It all looked fine in the brochure but they seem to be making it up as they go along.

Woman: Yes, I mean, the excursions! I always wanted to go to those places and *they* haven't let me down, but all that waiting around!

Man: Still, I guess you can't really expect much better for the money, can you?

PAUSE 2 SECONDS - REPEAT - PAUSE 2 SECONDS

7   *You receive a telephone call. Who's phoning?*
     A   *a representative of a telephone company*
     B   *a local journalist*
     C   *a telephone repair engineer*

PAUSE 5 SECONDS

Hello, I wonder if I could just take up a few moments of your time? We're conducting a survey into what people think of the telephone service in this area and I'd just like to ask you a few questions about what you're satisfied and dissatisfied with – especially with regard to the prompt repair of faults. We'll be publishing the results and we'll be acting on them so that you get a better service ...

PAUSE 2 SECONDS - REPEAT - PAUSE 2 SECONDS

8   *You hear someone talking at a party. What is he talking about?*
     A   *a new TV channel*
     B   *a new TV programme*
     C   *a new TV star*

PAUSE 5 SECONDS

Yes, it was the first time I'd seen it, and I couldn't believe it. I mean, it's all so amateur! The presenters keep looking at the wrong cameras, and there's one who has an interview programme and he just hasn't got a clue what he's doing – I gather they've decided to get rid of him. Where do they get them from? All those adverts about it being 'A New Kind of Television' – well, I suppose it is – it's worse than all the rest.

PAUSE 2 SECONDS - REPEAT - PAUSE 2 SECONDS

That is the end of Part 1. Now turn to Part 2.

PART 2

You will hear part of a radio programme in which postcards are discussed. For questions 9–18, complete the sentences.

You now have 45 seconds in which to look at Part 2.

PAUSE 45 SECONDS

Presenter: Well, postcards are so much a part of everyday life that it's hard to imagine a time when they didn't exist. Well, from tomorrow until the end of the month there's an exhibition celebrating the history of the British picture postcard at the Royal Exhibition Centre, and our reporter, Sally Wells, is there.

Sally: Yes, thanks David. This exhibition has been organized by the Postcard Traders' Association and 100 dealers from all over the world have gathered to display about 2 million cards. I have with me Neil Parkhouse, chairman of the Association. Neil, when did postcards start?

Neil: Well, the first postcards in Britain went on sale in 1870, but they were blank. The Post Office first allowed the use of picture postcards in 1894. They had room for only the briefest of messages - words had to be written on the same side as the picture, leaving the back for the address and stamp. The golden age of the postcard didn't begin until this restriction was lifted in 1902, when the 'divided back' was allowed - this meant that the picture was on the front and the back was split in half - half for the words and half for the address and stamp, as today. This meant that publishers were free to explore a vast range of subject material and as a result, one of the first collecting crazes of the Twentieth Century - known as deltiology - started.

Sally: So they caught on straight away?

Neil: Yes, in the next six years, one hundred million postcards were sold in Britain. Many were never used but were put straight into albums by people who were collecting them. Millions more were used to send simple messages. In fact, postal deliveries were so quick and reliable that one businessman who made the daily trip to London from his home fifty kilometres away would send a postcard to his wife, telling her what time he would be home.

Sally: Has collecting postcards always been a popular hobby?

Neil: Well, in the middle part of the century the postcard declined quite considerably, because of increases in postage rates, greater use of the telephone, and changing social habits, and this was reflected in a fall in postcard collecting. In the 1950s, comic postcards and those with countryside views were the only ones people collected. But in the 1960s, there was a huge revival of interest in collecting, and this continues today.

Sally: So what's the appeal of collecting postcards today?

Neil: There are a variety of reasons. In the first place, many postcards are miniature works of art, giving visual pleasure. But there's also the historical value. Local historians are very interested in topographical views - street scenes - which show them how towns and villages used to be, and enable them to compare them with how they are now. These postcards show how society was in the past. At the beginning of the Twentieth Century, postcards were commonly used as an early form of news reporting - the postcard at that time was actually a photographic record - remember, there weren't photos in newspapers and magazines then.

Sally: And are some of these postcards worth a lot of money?

Neil: They can be. There are albums of pictures which people have long forgotten about, which hold absolute treasures, all over the country. Some rare postcards can be worth hundreds, even thousands, of pounds.

Sally: So, David, perhaps you'd better check whether you've got a valuable postcard or two lying around in your house!

Presenter: I will. Thanks, Sally. That was Sally Wells, reporting from the postcard exhibition at ...

PAUSE 10 SECONDS

Now you will hear Part 2 again.

REPEAT - PAUSE 5 SECONDS

That is the end of Part 2. Now turn to Part 3.

PART 3

You will hear five different people talking about a famous sportsman who has retired. For questions 19-23, choose from the list A-F who each speaker is. Use the letters only once. There is one extra letter which you do not need to use.

You now have 30 seconds in which to look at Part 3.

PAUSE 30 SECONDS

Speaker 1 He's one of the all-time greats. I knew the first time I saw him that he was going to be something special. I've followed his career from the start and it's been great watching him. Of course, a lot's been written about him, and not all of it good, and he's certainly had his share of arguments with the people who run the game. But for those of us who love the team, he's given us a tremendous amount of joy. Going to matches won't be quite the same without him playing.

PAUSE 2 SECONDS

Speaker 2 Every country needs its heroes and he's certainly been one of ours. I can't pretend he was always that easy to get on with during games - he was quite an opponent, I can tell you, but once the game was over, he was always the first one to come over for a laugh and a chat. He'll certainly be missed - crowds loved him.

PAUSE 2 SECONDS

Speaker 3 I suppose we didn't always see eye to eye on matters of discipline, but there's no doubt he's been good for the sport. He seemed to think that we treated him like a naughty schoolboy - all those fines we gave him and all that - but I suppose from our point of view he was a bit of a trouble-maker. But he was great to watch and he certainly brought the crowds in.

PAUSE 2 SECONDS

Speaker 4 A lot of my colleagues found it hard to get on with him but I always found him very approachable. I suppose he got fed up with some of the things that were said about him, and that made him suspicious of talking to people like me. But as the years went by, I built up a good relationship with him and I think he came to realize that I wasn't going to make up things he was supposed to have said, like some of the others do.

PAUSE 2 SECONDS

Speaker 5 From an early age it was clear to me that he was going to succeed - in sport, that is. Nothing else mattered to him, and that could be annoying for me at times, I must admit. I could never get him to do anything I wanted him to do and he never seemed to be listening. But in games he could concentrate and he was certainly a winner. He couldn't wait to leave, I guess - he obviously thought it was all a waste of time and he just wanted to get on with playing.

PAUSE 10 SECONDS

Now you will hear Part 3 again.

REPEAT - PAUSE 5 SECONDS

That is the end of Part 3. Now turn to Part 4.

PART 4

You will hear part of a radio programme about people's jobs. For questions 24-30, choose the best answer A, B or C.

You now have one minute in which to look at Part 4.

PAUSE 1 MINUTE

Announcer: In today's programme about people and their jobs, we hear from Nick Butler, who is a Tour Leader for High Adventure Holidays, and Alison Gray, the Managing Director of the company he works for.

Nick: When I first left school, I was all set for a conventional career - I was pushed into studying accountancy because that's where my basic skills were at the time. After starting to travel I realized, I think, that my future would lie in tourism and so I changed to a tourism course. I thought it would be a good move. During the third year of the course, we had to work in the tourism industry and to do that I decided to apply to various adventure tour operators. One of them contacted me and said I was suited to work as a Tour Leader in Egypt and that was it!

Alison: The sort of person who wants to be a Tour Leader on adventure holidays is one of probably two particular personalities - either the sort of person who wants to travel and is outgoing and therefore sees this as a vehicle to allow them to travel - or, they're going to be the sort of person that just likes working with people. The kind of qualifications that are needed are a bit difficult to define. There are no set requirements - knowing foreign languages is preferable, getting on with people is essential, travel experience is beneficial. Clearly if I've got two candidates to choose from and one has done a lot of travelling, the person who's travelled the more will be more likely to get the job - but even that is not essential. You shouldn't put somebody off if they haven't travelled at all, because in essence if their personality is right, they're suitable.

Nick: We have to do a lot of research prior to departure to the destination, uh, that usually involves two or three weeks, perhaps even four weeks, a lot of which is spent in libraries, buying guide books, reading about the history of the country, local cultures, food, and so on, so you really need to know everything about the country and be able to answer any questions the groups might have.

Alison: You need somebody who is not at all self-centred. It's got to be understood if you go in for this sort of work that you're going into a service industry. The fact is, if you go on holiday with 16 people, the 16 people are important because they need you to look after them. Your interests come second.

Nick: You need to have good organizational skills obviously, to deal with so many different possible logistics, such as meeting times, train departure times, you might have to pick up a taxi when a train arrives or a bus, everything's got to be spot-on and working smoothly, because one minor hiccup might cost you a day of the itinerary. Organization has got to be really spot-on all the time.

Alison: The sort of tour leaders that we look for are very different I think from the package tour courier, shall we say. The sort of tours that we run, because they go off the beaten track, because they're being operated in remote areas, many of the logistical arrangements are in the hands of the tour leader and he or she is inevitably with the group all the time - it's a twenty-four hours a day job. That means you need a different type of person, they've got to be more at ease with the idea of having people with them all the time.

Nick: Sometimes you can get a bit tired of the travelling, travelling out of a suitcase or backpack - moving from one place to another every one night or two nights can become a bit tedious - but you eventually get into a set routine, where you can pack your bag in two or three minutes and move on. And you can just blot it out, and every room you get in different hotels, every different tent, is like home to you for that period of time. Loneliness also can be a distinct downside, because quite often you have to keep a distance from the group, the group members, there's often things you'd like to be talking to people about, but because you're in the position you are, you can't suddenly go and talk to a group member about your problems, you have to bottle them up and absorb them all yourself.

Within the tour leader field you can expand obviously in experience - the higher you get in your field, the better destinations you get to lead tours in, and the higher salary you get, of course. After tour leading, you can move into the office, into office-based work, either into operations or marketing.

What I think really pleases me about the job, one of the things I get out of it, is at the end of the tour when the group turns around to you and says 'We've had a great holiday, Nick, a great tour, thanks very much' and give you a pat on the back - and some groups give you a present. These are memories that you can keep forever, that are really nice and really mean a lot to you. You've got to basically ensure that everyone has a satisfactory holiday and has a great time and wants to book again with the company.

PAUSE 10 SECONDS

Now you will hear Part 4 again.

REPEAT - PAUSE 5 SECONDS

That is the end of Part 4.

There will now be a pause of five minutes for you to copy your answers onto the separate answer sheet. Your supervisor will then collect all the question papers and answer sheets.